Dogmanese
for
Daydreamers

The Author

Ian McMurdo was born in May 1949, the son of a coal miner. He was brought up in New Cumnock, Ayrshire. When he was four years old, he moved with his family to a council housing scheme in nearby Logan Toll.

He was educated in Lugar Primary School, Cumnock Academy, Strathclyde University, then Jordanhill College of Education, Glasgow, from which he emerged in 1972 as a qualified chemistry teacher. After sixteen years in the teaching profession, Ian moved into local government management and was appointed Director of Education for West Dunbartonshire Council in 1995. Having served nine years at the helm, he took voluntary early retirement to set up his own management consultancy business, which he operates in partnership with 'a few trusted colleagues'.

Ian still lives in the Cumnock area with his wife Nan and their beloved Labrador retrievers, Tanna and Saffy. Ian and Nan have two grown-up children, Jillian and Derek, and one granddaughter, Anna. The family also has a holiday home in Kildonan, on the southernmost tip of the island of Arran, which is their favourite place on earth.

Ian is a well-known educational commentator, public speaker, Burns enthusiast and occasional journalist. His first book, *A Life Worth Living*, was published by Carn Publishing in April 2010, and immediately became a bestseller, selling out within six weeks.

Dogmanese For Daydreamers is Ian's second book.

Dögmanese for Daydreamers

Ian McMurdo

CARN PUBLISHING

©Ian McMurdo, 2010.
First Published in Great Britain, 2010.

ISBN – 978 0 9518128 9 1

Published by Carn Publishing,
Lochnoran House,
Auchinleck, Ayrshire, KA18 3JW.

Printed by Bell & Bain Ltd.,
Glasgow, G46 7UQ.

Dogmanese For Daydreamers is dedicated to my wonderful family; my wife Nan, our two children Jillian and Derek, their spouses Paul and Catriona, and our new baby granddaughter Anna.

However, even they will understand that I wrote this book especially for my five magnificent big dogs, Cindy, Katy and Meg who are sadly no longer with us, and Tanna and Saffy who are thankfully still by my side to this very day. To their considerable collective *chagrin*, but in deference to the intellectual limitations of the human race, I have written this book in mere words and sentences and paragraphs and chapters.

And if you read on, you might actually begin to understand just how really amusing our canine friends consider that to be.

Ian McMurdo
October 2010

By the same author

A Life Worth Living

Acknowledgements

In writing *Dogmanese for Daydreamers*, I found the following publications to be very helpful and informative. I would recommend both to anyone with a keen interest in human-canine communication and behavioural psychology.

Bruce Fogle, *The Dog's Mind*, Pelham Books,
Stephen Greene Press, 1990.

Stanley Coren, *How To Speak Dog*, Free Press,
Simon & Schuster, New York, 2000.

The poem *Heaven's Gate* was inspired by
The Rainbow Bridge (Author Unknown)

Contents

Prologue : Bess's Tale

*'I prefer the company of animals more than the company of humans.
To be merciless is the privilege of civilised humans.'
(Sigmund Freud, Founder of Psychoanalysis)*

I was only ten years old when I first decided that I wanted a dog. My mind was made up one bitter cold afternoon just before Christmas in 1959. It was the easiest decision I would ever make, although it would take another fifteen years to bring to fruition.

As I sat at my old wooden school desk, watching the lanky, bespectacled Mrs Ferguson painstakingly replenish the contents of my neatly recessed inkwell from a big bottle of *Quink* ink, I cast yet another glance across the room towards my best mate, Danny. His eyes were red and blotchy, and the tears still trickled gently down his cheeks, as they had done more or less all day. Words could not describe the sympathy I felt for Danny that afternoon, nor my revulsion at the heinous misdeed that had caused his anguish.

The previous evening, we had been playing football with the other local worthies on the tarmac road under the only fully-operational streetlight in a small council housing scheme in Logan Toll, in the coal mining heartland of Ayrshire. As usual, the two sets of goalposts were constructed from an assortment of torn schoolbags, crumpled school blazers and darned jumpers. The raised pavements provided the shy-lines, thus perfectly circumscribing the parameters of our hallowed arena, which our over-imaginative young minds had convinced ourselves was a replica of Hampden Park, Scotland's world-famous national football stadium. On this particular occasion, Danny was in my team. Thankfully.

We always picked our teams by the 'cock-or-a-hen' methodology of the 'fifties. Political correctness hadn't been invented yet, but life went on nevertheless. Danny was invariably picked first, an absolutely unavoidable outcome as his signature on a professional contract for West Bromwich Albion would testify a few years later. If Danny was on your side, you won, plain and simple. The downside was that the burst ball with which we were playing would be tied to his dazzling feet all evening as the rest of us ran about mesmerised, hoping against hope to get a kick at the bloody thing. Danny was a football genius, no more and no less. He also happened to be salt of the earth.

'Danny, yer tea's ready!' It was his Uncle Jock who was the bearer of that particular evening's unwelcome news, which signalled the end of the match.

'Can Ian come in, Uncle Jock?' Danny enquired.

'Aye, but has he had his tea? There's no' enough mince in the pot.'

'Aye Mr Harrison, I've had ma tea,' I replied immediately, in the certain knowledge that, depleted mince supplies notwithstanding, I would get playing with Bess while Danny, his Uncle Jock and his Grandpa were eating theirs.

'Fifteen-six for us, ya beauty!' I shouted clenched-fisted to the opposition, as I ran up the overgrown garden path towards Danny's semi-detached council house.

'We'll get ye back the morn, ya specky bastards,' came the truculent reply, not-too-subtly referring to the fact that both Danny and I were of the four-eyed persuasion.

From the age of three, Danny had been brought up by his Grandpa and his Uncle Jock, in the aftermath of his own father having been tragically mown down as he staggered out of the Temple Bar one summer's afternoon into the path of an oncoming National Coal Board lorry. I never really knew how his mother's life progressed after that, but somehow I just instinctively knew that it would not have been a particularly comfortable conversation topic.

Both Jock and the old man were coal miners, along with almost every other male in the village. I vividly remember how the two of them used to strip to their vests of an evening and scrub their faces, forearms and hands in the kitchen sink before preparing the dinner. That night was no exception, at least insofar as the scrubbing routine went. However, there was something different in the air, something very strange.

'Right, get sat doon boy,' Danny's Grandpa said brusquely. 'Dae ye think that a' I've got tae dae is graft doon the pit a' day, make the dinner an' wait fur you tae feenish playin' that silly gemme o' fitba? Ye get things far too easy these days, boy. It was never like this in ma day.'

I remember feeling really uneasy that particular evening, very jumpy. There was tension in the air, no doubt about it. I could smell it. It was almost as clearly discernible as the contents of the two plates the old man was carrying towards the table in the living room, which constituted mince, potatoes and cabbage, each plate adorned by an enormous slimy doughball.

Nobody spoke a word, not a single word. Despite the intense negative polarity in the room, I continued to play with Danny's dog Bess. She was a small black-and-gold mongrel with a beautiful, pointed face, long soft ears and a docked tail. Bess's toy was a rolled-up page of the Daily Express, which I would throw across the room for her to chase. Every time I threw it, she would bring it back to me with what remained of the stump of her tail wagging furiously. She really was a clever little soul, and such a happy dog. I adored Bess, but not as much as Danny did. He was simply in love with her.

I heard his Grandpa coming back into the living room. He bellowed just two words. 'Move, you!'

I froze with fear.

Thankfully, it was Bess he was talking to, not me. He was carrying his own dinner plate. Bess stared at him, but just stood there waiting for me to throw the newspaper-cum-toy. As he walked towards her, he swung his hefty miner's foot with enormous force, and booted Bess full blast in the stomach. The poor little thing howled in agony and catapulted a good four feet through the air, crash-landing with her head in the fireplace and her backside in the blazing coal fire. She got up, still howling, and bolted out the back door towards her kennel in the back garden. I can still vividly remember the acrid stench of her hair singeing on the red-hot coals.

Danny and Uncle Jock just sat there, staring at their mince-and-tatties, and said absolutely nothing. Not a word. They had seen it all before. However, I had not.

I ran out the door after Bess, who by this time was lying in her kennel in the freezing cold, shaking uncontrollably and whimpering helplessly. Till the day I die, I'll never forget the pleading, terrified look on her little face. I cradled her in my arms and started sobbing. And then, to my eternal shame, I ran all the way home.

The next morning, Danny found Bess lying dead in her kennel with blood pouring out of her anus. We never really spoke much about it and I never told a soul. Until now, that is. Perhaps I could have saved Bess, but I will never know, will I? That thought has haunted me for almost half a century.

However, from that day forth, I vowed that some day soon I would get a big dog of my own and treat it properly. I also realised that I would have to know for sure if I actually was treating it properly.

And that's why I invented *Dogmanese.*

The Loneliness Of The Dogless Child

'Whenever a man loves a dog, he derives great power from it.'
(Chief Dan George, Sioux Indian Tribe)

Old Man Time has a lot to answer for, don't you think? I used to laugh when I heard adults saying that time speeds up when you get older. How vividly I remember my near-eighty-year-old grandfather giving me a little pep talk just before I began my University career in the late 1960s.

'Work hard, try your best and enjoy every minute of it son, because life's far too short. And get your hair cut, because you look like a big lassie.'

Try as I might, I simply could not comprehend how someone who had lived as many years as the dear old man himself could in any possible way have come to the conclusion that life is too short. That view was further accentuated when my fresher year at Uni, in the bright lights of Glasgow, seemed to drag on for ever. In hindsight, I suppose that having a pretty girlfriend waiting patiently for me back home in Ayrshire might have had something to do with it. These days, however, and with the dubious benefit of six decades of reflection behind me, I can now truly appreciate what my grandfather had meant, particularly since I have witnessed the days accelerate exponentially over the latter part of my very fortunate life.

When I think back on the fifteen-year period between Bess's tragic death and the eventual acquisition of my own very first dog, it seemed like an eternity. In all likelihood, that was probably on account of this relativity thing, where time appears to forge ahead much faster in our advancing years than it does in one's childhood. How Albert Einstein missed that one is quite beyond me.

There is absolutely no doubt in my mind that I would have grown up to be a much more insightful and reflective young adult if I had been brought up with a dog in the family during my childhood years. In no way do I fault my parents for depriving me of canine company during these formative years. God knows that with my father working his arse off for seven quid a week, six days a week down a coal mine and my mother the harassed but superb homemaker, they were struggling badly enough just to feed the humans in the family without a dog eating them out of house and home. It was simply that I was a particularly lonely child and an individual who, still to this very day, often finds it difficult to connect with others on an emotional level. Except with the chosen very few, that is, and only they will know who I'm talking about.

The horrific fate of Bess heralded something of a watershed for me, I suppose. Quite simply, it was time for little Ian to start growing up. I had witnessed real violence and cruelty for the first time in my young life, my primary school days were drawing to a close and the 'big' school was beckoning at the end of the next summer. Worse still, I would soon necessarily become parted from my bosom buddy Danny, on account of the notorious 'streaming' methodology of the post-war era which involved placing children into school class groups according to their general 'academic ability', whatever that was supposed to be. While Danny and I were both relatively bright young creatures, the streaming system would still conspire to keep us apart, and it would be another decade or so until the penny would drop with our political masters that children's education, social development and life chances could be made all the richer from properly differentiated approaches to mixed-ability learning and teaching.

And so the halcyon days of handcraft, needlework, searching for acorns in the adjacent autumnal forests and singing *The Big Rock Candy Mountain* at the top of our high-pitched voices whilst waiting for our testicles to drop into our underpants, were slowly but surely drawing to a premature close, soon to be replaced by algebra, geometry, trigonometry and groping girls' developing bosoms in the bicycle shed.

'Just think of the new friends you'll meet', our rather effeminate teacher Mr Thomas had told us on our last day in primary school. Very few of us had been convinced, particularly since Danny and I had met a first year pupil from the local secondary school only a few days earlier, when we had been perched on our bikes at the top of the Peasie Brae, the very steep road from which our beloved and late lamented primary school was accessed.

'Twa things will happen tae ye in yer first year,' the little sprat had gleefully informed us.

'Tae stert wae, when the playtime bell rings on yer first day, aboot a dozen big third year boys will grab ye and take ye intae the toilet block, and shove yer heid doon the lavvy. They'll then gie ye yer dumps, which means thumpin' ye on the back wae their fists, so that ye cannae breath while yer heid's under the pishy water. When ye pass oot, they normally let ye go, but six first years drooned this year, so they did. And they say that, next year, the third year boys are real nutters, so I wid watch oot if I wiz yooz.'

'And w-w-h-h-i-i-t-t's the second thing?' I asked in frozen terror, as a big yellow puddle appeared below my Raleigh bicycle pedals.

'Aw, that's yer TB jag,' our elder counsellor replied. 'Ye have tae staun' in a big long queue ootside the medical room fur ages an' ages, waitin' yer turn, and that's wan o' the worst bits, because ye can see the first years being dragged oot screamin'. Apart fae the wans that huv already fainted. They get cairried oot oan a streetcher, so they dae.'

'Is it s-s-s-sair?' asked Danny, hyperventilating. 'The jag?'

'IS IT SAIR?' came the booming rhetorical question, accompanied by a howl of wicked laughter. 'It makes me greet jist tae think aboot it!' he replied, somewhat less than reassuringly.

'When your turn comes, they tell ye tae roll up yer shirt sleeve. Then twae big nurses grab ye in a heidlock and anither yin peens yer hauns behin' yer back, so that ye cannae move, so ye cannae. The doaktur then takes oot his huge big needle an' fills it fou o' yon green stuff that's bubblin' an' smokin' an' stinkin'. I think they ca' it sulfakloarick acid or somethin' like that. Then he shoves the needle intae yer airm. I'm no' sure whit happens next, because I passed oot at that bit, but when I came roon' the needle wiz a' the way up ma airm fae ma elbow tae ma shooder, wae only the haundle stickin' oot. He then twisted it yin way then the ither, until the point o' it burst oot ma shooder. That wiz when he telt the nurse that it hudnae worked richt, an' he wid need tae dae the hale thing a' ower again oan the ither airm.'

'An', ... d-d-d-did he?' I enquired, almost unable to breath.

'Aye, but I cannae remember the rest, 'cos I passed oot again, an' woke up in the hoaspital aboot teatime. But I've still goat the scabs tae prove it.'

'Can I s-s-s-e-e-e them?' asked Danny, gasping for air.

'Naw,' came the sombre reply, 'I widnae want tae scare ye.'

I vividly recall going home and incarcerating myself in my bedroom for the great bulk of the ensuing months between the end of the current school session and the beginning of the next. Any time I mentioned our conversation-on-the-bike to my ultra-pragmatic parents, they merely laughed it off and told me that the little upstart had been exaggerating. I remember thinking that if he had only exaggerated his account of both procedures by a mere factor of ten thousand, then the experiences would still be absolutely hellish.

However, I also remember wishing that I had someone really nice to talk to about this, and about other things. Someone who would really listen to me, and who would simply look into my eyes and tell me that everything would turn out fine. Even at that age, I knew without the merest shadow of a doubt that the only 'person' who could perform this task was a big dog, and I would have walked barefoot on burning coals just to have one lying on my bed beside me.

The twenty four hours immediately preceding my introduction to secondary school lasted approximately three days, not including night-time. I was absolutely petrified, not just at the prospect of drowning in gallons of adolescent urine, although that specific thought was not a particularly appealing one, but mainly because of the dramatic disappearance of the psychological security that I had come to rely upon all the way through my previous seven years at primary school. I didn't eat a thing all day. When my parents asked me what was wrong, I just said I wasn't feeling very well, but I'm sure they knew the real reason. Before I went to bed, I packed my new pens, pencils, ruler, set squares and compasses into my new schoolbag, and vomited violently into the toilet pan.

I simply couldn't get to sleep, other than for a few minutes here and there, and every single horrific thought imaginable ran riot in my hyperactive cerebrum. It was at three-thirty precisely that I decided there was nothing else for it, and I did what I knew I had to do.

I invented my own dog.

She was beautiful, golden-brown in colour and she was called Meg. She had lovely big ears and a long furry tail. Tellingly, however, she possessed the most piercing brown eyes that I just knew would watch over me for eternity. Meg was born not as a spontaneous consequence of the reproductive process that I had been reading about in my Sunday School booklet, but out of deep psychological necessity. I would take care of her for ever, and she would always protect me from whatever adolescent life dared to throw at me. She would be our own little secret and nobody would ever need to know about her. Every time I went out to play, I would sneak her out along with me and I would always keep two plates in my room for her, one for food and the other for water. If my mother asked where the plates were, I would just have to tell a little white lie and say that I had dropped them while I was drying the dishes.

'Meg, I'm really worried about school tomorrow,' I whispered in her ear. Meg looked at me, but her mouth said nothing in reply. It was her big intelligent brown eyes that spoke to me.

'There's nothing to worry about, Ian,' they said. 'Secondary school will be great fun. And you'll meet a lot of new pals. And you'll still see Danny at playtimes.'

'But what about the third years giving me my dumps and sticking my head down the lavvy pan?' I asked her nervously.

And Meg replied, 'You can take me to school with you tomorrow, if you like. Nobody will ever notice me. Unless they try to give you your dumps, that is. Then I'll rip their nuts off.'

I giggled for the first time that whole day. 'Okay, then, you can come with me if you like. Night, night, Meg.'

'Night, night, Ian. Now let's get some kip, because we've got a big day ahead of us tomorrow.'

At that point she snuggled up beside me, and we both fell deeply asleep.

The following morning in the playground, I met Danny and a few other primary school mates who were wearing the same petrified facial expressions as no doubt I was sporting. However, at least I had Meg by my side as my minder, on her invisible blue lead. They had nobody to look out for them.

Amazingly, my first day at secondary school came and went, and my drowning-in-piss virginity remained intact. A few weeks later, the TB jag transpired to be nothing more than a little prick, which I must say turned out to be a very accurate description for the despicable urchin who had ruined my entire summer holidays, on account of his highly imaginative tales of terror.

Much to my surprise, I rather enjoyed secondary school. First of all, there were the enormous range and diversity of subjects, from the fascinating world of truly practical experiences like woodwork, metalwork and art, to the more cerebral challenges of mathematics and the sciences that would go on to form the basis of my professional studies some six testosterone-charged and zit-infested years later. Then there was the choice of umpteen new sporting activities, ranging from gymnastics and swimming through to rugby and basketball. Football would always be my own particular favourite sport, although our vertically-challenged physical education teacher kept reminding us that rugby was the only real man's sport and that 'football is just a game for big jessies with squeaky voices and saggy breasts.' Even although it was 1961 by now, political correctness had still not arrived, and we all kept wondering when it was due to make its welcome appearance.

As time went on, I no longer felt the need to take Meg with me to school, and left her sleeping cosily on my bed each day until I alighted from the four o'clock school bus to be greeted with big licks on the cheeks and a wagging tail, after which the two of us would sneak out to play before teatime. It would be another forty years until I got my real Meg, and only another six after that until my heart would be broken when I would lose her for ever through cancer.

I really don't remember all that much else about my adolescent years, other than that it seemed to become increasingly easier to pee out of the skylight window than to aim the relevant appendage into the urinal, particularly after Cathy Kirby's magnificent bosoms had tried their best to pop out of her low-cut frock on *Sunday Night At The London Palladium*. I always dreaded 'the discussion' with my father, which we had all been assured by our Sunday School teacher would occur any day now, but it never did. Thankfully.

I do, however, remember my mother saying to me one evening, 'Ian, do you need to know anything about …… well ……. things?'

'What things, mum?' I replied innocently.

'Oh, things about growing up ………. and how to make babies ………. and how to prevent having babies ………. and things like that.'

'Naw, it's okay,' I replied, as my complexion changed from infra-scarlet to ultra-beetroot. 'They gave us a wee book at Sunday School.'

'Oh right, ……. good. That's fine then. Just remember that if you want to know anything else, you can talk to ……….. you can ask ……….. your daddy!'

And that was that. Did she simply not realise that if I had

really wanted to find out about the relative merits and demerits of penises, breasts and menstrual cycles, my own father would have been the very last person on planet earth that I would have asked? I honestly would much rather have had that particular discussion with a serial axe murderer whose chosen next victim was to be a highly-impressionable, bespectacled twelve-year-old. So I went back up to my bedroom, read the booklet again and discussed it with my loyal Meg.

The local Sunday School was easily the most unintentionally sexual forum in which I had ever been involved, and that even included my Biology lessons at school. This was principally on account of the assorted party games we played, such as Postman's Knock, during one of which I experienced my very first climax, on the occasion of a delectable young blonde thing who called herself Nancy pulling me into the cupboard and giving me a French kiss. I honestly thought that my trousers had exploded.

It's a funny thing, but my most vivid memories of key moments in my teens are inextricably associated with the wonderful music of the early sixties. To this very day, if I hear a song of that era on the radio, it inevitably triggers a crystal-clear image of what was going on at the time in my youthful, if often troubled mind.

'I Wanna Hold Your Hand' by *The Beatles* evokes very powerful memories of my desire to ask Nancy out on a date, but I neither had the confidence nor the courage to do so, and anyway what would I have done if she actually did hold my hand and I erupted yet again in my co-op underpants?

'California Girls' by *The Beach Boys* aroused many an erotic image, if somewhat frustratingly devoid of detail, in my overcharged young brain. 'I'm A Believer' by *The Monkees* still reminds me of lying on Ayr beach with some school buddies on a beautiful summer's day, watching the world and a succession of lovely giggling girls go by. 'Monday Monday' by *The Mamas And The Papas* makes me think of a rainy evening in the Coffee Mill in Cumnock's Glaisnock Street, and '24 Hours From Tulsa' still grates on my brain to such an extent that it makes me want to trash *Gene Pitney's* car. On the other hand, 'Norwegian Wood' by *The Beatles* was, and remains, the best and most evocative song ever to cross my consciousness.

TV commercials still have that same nostalgic effect on me. How vividly I remember sitting in my pyjamas with a glass of milk and a digestive biscuit, beside my mum, dad and younger sister, watching *Opportunity Knocks* being presented by Hughie Green, when the commercial break would be heralded by a big star-shaped image flashing onto the black-and-white screen.

'The Esso sign means happy motoring, Call in for Esso Extra, call in for Esso Extra.'

Lyrics to die for.

I used to sing these songs, and even some of the commercial jingles as well, to Meg before going to sleep, until one night when I was about fifteen she said to me, 'For God's sake Ian, put a bloody sock in it and switch on Radio Caroline instead.'

Meg and I were never quite the same after that, and as we began to need each other's attention less and less, we slowly started to drift apart. The end came when I said to her one day, 'I'm sorry Meg, but it's a real dog I need now, not some stupid figment of my imagination.'

And she replied, 'Aye, and what I need is a real master, not some plooky, four-eyed adolescent.'

Then in an instant, she simply disappeared into the ether and I simultaneously became immersed in an ocean of pure testosterone, from which it would take me several years to escape. However, when I did eventually scramble out onto the sands of maturity, a real dog would be there waiting for me.

Her name would be Cindy, and she would save me from a life of self-pity and hopelessness.

Our Love Affair With Canis Familiaris

*'If an animal does something, we call it instinct; if we do the same thing for
the same reason, we call it intelligence.'*
(Will Cuppy, Journalist and Humourist)

Now, let's establish one very important matter from the
outset, and that is this.

I am not a veterinary surgeon-turned-writer. In fact, I am
not a vet at all when I come to think about it. Nor indeed do I
have any pretensions whatsoever about being an animal
behavioural expert. Neither do I aspire, in any shape or form,
to emulate those massed ranks of famed canine experts, many
or all of whose names you might care to reel off by heart, and all
of whom could tie me in knots with their knowledge of Border
Collies' left ventricles, German Shepherds' right testicles and
Shih Tzus' anal discharges.

No folks, I am a dog lover, plain and simple. And, into the
bargain, one who has been fortunate enough to have had five
magnificent big canine soulmates into the bargain. And thus it
is with these few modest introductory words of uncharacteristic
self-effacement, that I present this completely non-scientific
account of the fascinating world of *Canis Familiaris* who is,
without the merest shadow of a doubt, my very best friend on
planet earth.

That having been said, however, in comparison with the
hordes of assorted celebrities and many, many others who might
justifiably lay claim to possessing some form of expert canine
knowledge, I do have one particularly notable thing going for
me, and that is this. I can speak *Dogmanese*, and they cannot.

Do allow me to explain.

You see, *Homo Sapien* believes itself to be the supreme being on this planet of ours. The top of the evolutionary tree, or the king of the jungle if you will. And there are many reasons for this rather quaint belief.

We can think logically, and speak, read and write in hundreds of different languages, thousands in fact. We can ride a bicycle, drive a double-decker bus and sail a fishing boat. We can fly a Tornado jet plane. We can invent antibiotics, perform life-saving surgery and transplant vital organs. We can develop global technology and communicate to all four corners of the planet by telephone or through the internet. We can put men, women and monkeys on the moon. Indeed, if someone from a far-off land pisses us off, not only can we phone them up and have it out with them there and then, but we can instead have a cup of tea, then send them an intercontinental ballistic thermonuclear missile and obliterate their entire country. All in all, we really are a species of right little clever clogs. At least, so we believe.

So what's all this got to do with our friend, the dog, I hear you ask? Well, quite a lot actually. You see, as the unrivalled smarty-pants that we all believe ourselves to be, we have the arrogance to lie back on our posh recliners and observe other animals' behaviour with a rather knowing gaze, an activity with which we are particularly obsessed, in the deeply misguided belief that they are more primitive than we are in almost every single regard.

However, to be fair and balanced about it, we also obsess in observing the behaviour of our own species. And that is why we drool over topical magazines like *Hello* and *Nuts*, and why we become so hopelessly addicted to reality TV programmes like *Who Wants to be a Millionaire?* and *Big Brother*. That's also why we're so hell-bent on finding out who's got a new three-piece suite, or the latest Vauxhall Viagra model and, even more importantly, who's sleeping with the postman. As a species, we are utterly infatuated with observing other people's and other animals' behaviour. In fact, it is our favourite pastime.

However, we do so with a rather sinister and somewhat superior attitude. We love to watch the neighbour's cat chase a mouse up and down the garden, or play with the curtain cord. We are fascinated by a robin having a wash in the garden birdbath, or swaying on a branch whilst singing its little heart out. We love watching the local farmer's cow sticking its big stupid head over the hedge to greet us, or his hens darting around in no particular direction for no particular reason, or his pet pig snorting furiously as it shuffles its enormous backside towards us. We howl in wicked amusement in the local zoo, as the East African monkey masturbates feverishly for the seventh time that morning. No wonder his wrists are strong enough to propel him through the branches, we postulate. We constantly observe, compare and contrast animal behaviour with our own human traits.

Except, of course, when we're talking about our best friend, the dog.

You see, we don't simply observe our dogs, or compare and contrast them with ourselves. We actually try to programme their behaviour to make them the same as we are. We relate to them as 'part of the family'. We treat them as equals. We give them names, we buy them squeaky toys, we put fluffy blankets in their beds. We take them shopping, we go on holiday with them and we teach them tricks. They have their favourite films and television programmes. In compelling evidence, I once had a beautiful Golden Retriever called Katy, who would happily have sat all day mesmerised by *Tom and Jerry* but who, without a single moment's hesitation, would have bitten *Postman Pat's* arse off every time his little rotund face appeared on the box.

For reasons best known to ourselves, we spend our time wallowing in the quaint misapprehension that our brains are vastly superior to those of our canine friends, that we are much 'cleverer' than they are. And in a number of ways, we most certainly are. We can read the Sunday newspapers, play scrabble, write out the shopping list and calculate how much we owe the taxman. They, on the other hand, cannot, although my accountant Doreen did once tell me that my financial records looked as if the dogs had done the filing all by themselves.

However, let's not forget that their brains are programmed quite differently, and for good reason too. They could survive in the wild, wild woods for months on end, while you and I would struggle to cope for more than half an hour if Sky Plus went on the blink.

Dogs' powers of taste and smell are infinitely superior to ours. Have you ever seen a dog standing absolutely motionless with its snout raised, gently sniffing the air? He or she has probably just detected another dog, or perhaps merely a steak-and-ale pie, about half a mile away. Their powers of scent are utterly amazing. Today, my own two dogs, Tanna and Saffy, could tell immediately I returned home if I had actually stroked another dog half the length of the country away in downtown Doncaster. If I dropped a biscuit crumb, they would be fighting each other for it before it hit the carpet. If another dog had pissed on the back lawn at any time since the beginning of the last millennium, you could put your mortgage on them detecting it within three seconds. On the other hand, you and I couldn't sniff out a hot dame if she was sitting on the same settee.

My point? Comparing the intellectual capacities of *Homo Sapien* and *Canis Familiaris* is a totally meaningless exercise. It's akin to comparing oranges with lemons.

We are 'brighter' than they are. We can play Nintendo, programme computers and develop 3-D digital television. We can build new supermarkets, schools and hospitals. However, we can also start chemical wars, induce famine, permit genocide and fashion the near-total collapse of the world's financial markets. Dogs are nowhere near as skilled as us in such matters.

So, let us look at relative performance in terms of our execution of the five 'senses', shall we? This is what it all boils down to.

Sight:	*The dog wins*
Taste:	*The dog wins*
Smell:	*The dog wins*
Hearing:	*The dog wins*
Touch:	*Okay, we probably shade that one*

So there we have it, final score, 4 – 1 to the dog. Game, set and match.

So much, then, for the theory that our brains are superior to theirs. They are just different, that's all.

However, it's when it comes to the 'sixth sense' that the dog simply has no equal. Please permit me to tell you a really creepy story, but one which is completely authentic in every single detail.

One day recently on the island of Arran, our spiritual retreat just off the south-western coast of Scotland and where the family is fortunate enough to have a holiday home, I decided to take the two dogs a rather lengthy walk, first along the beach, then up through a wooded glen and finally back homewards along the main costal road. They had been roaming freely for the past two-and-a-half hours and, mercifully, both were getting a bit knackered by that time.

When I approached the wooden stile at the roadside, I put their leads back on again, and we began to stroll along the tarmac road towards the beautiful seaside village of Kildonan. After about ten minutes or so, we had reached a little hamlet in the country.

Suddenly, Tanna stopped in her tracks, with her jet-black hackles raised like a punk rocker's Mohican hairdo.

'Come on lass,' I said to her, but she was absolutely frozen to the spot. A team of wild horses couldn't have shifted her.

A moment later, Saffy's golden hackles did likewise, only in her case her lips curled too, which was most uncharacteristic.

At that point, the two of them started barking furiously, and I mean furiously. They were staring towards the bend in the road ahead of them and their barking continued with a ferocity I had never, ever witnessed before. I simply couldn't move them, and I actually thought about doing an abrupt U-turn and trying to go back home by another route. Just at that, their heads both started straining gradually to the left, with their barking continuing in the direction of their gazes, both sets of eyes turning very slowly in an anti-clockwise direction. They continued doing this until both of them were actually facing backwards in the direction from which we had just come. It really was as if an invisible being had just walked along the road beside us.

My skin crawled and a shiver ran up my spine. My scalp felt as if a small electric current was dancing on it. I gave another tug on the dogs' leads and, thankfully on this occasion, they again started walking to my side.

'Holy shit!' I remarked quietly to myself.

We turned the corner and the road developed into an S-bend, on the middle of which was a drystane dyke which formed the outer wall of a small bridge over a bubbling stream. At the foot of the wall lay a wreath of flowers. I thought nothing of it at the time, nothing at all.

When I reached Kildonan about twenty minutes later, I took the dogs down to the beach to give them a final swim, just to get the day's muck off their coats, thereby avoiding the inevitable scolding from my nearest-and-dearest.

As I walked into the house, my wife Nan's first words were, 'Ian, you'll never believe what happened earlier this morning. It's terrible. Jack's brother-in-law died in a car crash just up the road.'

I nearly shit myself.

Never, ever underestimate a dog's natural intelligence. Our canine friends might not be able to translate *Ulysses* into five contemporary languages, or rearrange a *Rubix* cube into perfect symmetry, but they possess powers of perception that you and I could only ever dream about.

And if you read on, I'll explain just how these incredible powers allow them to communicate, and to a remarkably sophisticated level at that, with mere *Homo Sapiens* like ourselves.

Bad Day In The Country

'Your dog is your only philosopher.'
(Plato, Greek Philosopher)

It was a beautiful summer's evening, almost seventeen years since I had made my pledge that, some day soon, I would get my own dog and treat it regally.

Now, for those of you who were kind enough to purloin my first book, *A Life Worth Living*, you will be forgiven if you think you have read about the following little tale before. However, so important was this particular tale to the development of our new and very secret language of *Dogmanese*, that I must now regale you with all of its gory detail. So here goes, get the hankies out of the drawer.

As I sat slumped in the driver's seat of my bright orange Ford Capri at Dalblair Bridge, a favourite country haunt in my earlier childhood days, a beautiful Golden Labrador sat opposite me in the passenger's seat, just staring at me as I sobbed uncontrollably. I stroked her magnificent forehead and reflected momentarily that I had actually looked after her pretty well since she had chosen to take up residence with us just under two years ago. What I hadn't realised until then was that it was she who would be looking after me that particular afternoon.

Nan and I had bought Cindy from a local farmer some nine months after we tied the knot. The fact that the timeframe was roughly equivalent to that of the human gestation period was entirely coincidental, since we hadn't even contemplated having a family until now, on account of our deployment of a very effective contraceptive device. It was called a mortgage repayment scheme. However, by now Nan was indeed pregnant, and we had been very happy with our lot. Until today, that was.

Before I continue with this rather life-changing tale, first please indulge me for a few moments, while I give you a little bit of the background.

Cindy had set me back the princely sum of ten pounds. It was to be the best tenner I would ever spend. She was the pick of her mother's litter of ten heavenly puppies, or to put it in another and more accurate way, she was Nan's pick.

As Mrs Donaldson, the farmer's wife, slid open the huge wooden barn door, they all bolted out in every conceivable direction. Cindy, however, made a beeline straight for Nan who immediately picked her up and refused to put her back down again. Half-an-hour later, our first ever puppy had been introduced to her new home. As she skipped inquisitively from room to room, Nan washed the puppy vomit from the pocket of her new Antartex coat. Cindy never did enjoy car travel.

Together, the three of us were a family blessed. These were the happiest days of my whole life and I just wish now that I had appreciated them more at the time. Nan and I were very much in love with each other, and with our new Andrex puppy, who immediately began to return that love many times over.

We spent a great deal of time together. Each morning before work, I would take Cindy out for a short walk while Nan made the tea and toast, and after we had both returned home from work in the late afternoon, we would plop her into the back seat of the car and take her to the local park. Most weekends, we would drive to the beach or to a quiet spot in the country where we would spend the entire time in hysterics at Cindy's antics. She was a mischievous little beggar, but a complete joy to behold, as the following few puppy anecdotes will testify.

On the evening of the 1974 Westminster general election, when she was only a few months old, Cindy plummeted from the top step of our staircase and landed on her back on the hall floor some twenty feet below, but lived to tell the tale. When the local vet arrived, his diagnosis decreed that Nan and I were in much greater need of medication than the pup herself. On one occasion, the ten-quid puppy ate precisely three times her market value in bank notes (five fivers and five singles, purely for the record), and on another she buried my spectacles in the vegetable patch of our back garden, some ten minutes before the Scotland v Zaire football match kicked off in the West Germany world cup finals. I would find them a fortnight later, by which time the Scots would have been sent homeward to think yet again.

On another occasion, she devoured the entire contents of a packet of heavy duty wallpaper paste, at which point yours truly decided to pour a pint of water over her throat. What a complete prick, my wife would helpfully counsel me, as our long-suffering vet scooped several buckets of paste out of her wretching gullet, thus avoiding her asphyxiation by a matter of seconds.

When left unattended, Cindy's party trick was to chew our furniture until the legs of the chairs and tables became pointed like pencils, and began to wobble. She ripped our embossed kitchen paper off the wall, one strip at a time, starting at the bottom and working carefully upwards towards the ceiling. One day, a mischievous teenager taunted her from outside the living room window, by rattling a stick against our cast-iron railing, and Cindy actually broke a pane of glass barking at him in exasperation. The poor lad was last seen leaping across our six-foot-high garden fence in a blind panic.

On yet another occasion, the postman inadvertently left the side gate open and Cindy wandered away from the house. We were beside ourselves with worry, but we needn't have bothered. A few minutes later, I saw her standing outside our big glass-fronted door. When I opened it, I couldn't believe my eyes. Her head, shoulders and front paws were completely covered in blood.

'Cindy!' I yelled, 'What's happened to you, lass?'

Nan immediately started crying, and draped her arms around her little pride and joy. I honestly thought that the poor thing had been hit by a car, or attacked by another dog. Then I noticed something in her mouth. When I tried to remove it, it scratched me. It was a small animal, a hedgehog in fact. All Cindy had wanted to do was bring us back a wee present, and she was quite prepared to rip her gums to shreds to afford us that privilege. Eventually, she released the hedgehog from her jaws and I placed the poor thing in the back garden from whence, five minutes later, it scurried away happily, no doubt in the direction from which it had come. The blood had all belonged to Cindy.

She really was our everything, our companion, our entertainer, our surrogate child at the time, I suppose.

And now, a couple of years later, here she was sitting in the car looking at my own big sorrowful eyes. Cindy had been born on a Christmas Day, and Nan and I had learned, much to our joy, that our first child had actually been conceived two Christmases later, with the big day expected around three months from now. However, only an hour ago, I had just learned something else too, and it was this that had devastated my whole world. It would soon devastate Nan's too, although she didn't know it quite yet.

Earlier that day, she had visited a local chiropractor who specialised in treating sports injuries, aching limbs, arthritic joints and things like that. Recently, she had begun to experience some very strange leg-related discomfort and spasms that were causing her a great deal of concern. Every now and again, her right leg would start trembling uncontrollably, and she had developed a bit of pain in her right hip and up into her spine. Even more worryingly, she had started to drag her right leg, and what had begun as a very faint limp had now developed into a much more pronounced walking defect.

Nan's local GP had told her that it was probably a condition called sciatica, which might have been caused by a trapped nerve in her spine, from which she would soon recover. The problem was that she couldn't have X-rays taken on her spinal column, due to her advanced pregnancy and the possible damage that radiation might cause to the foetus she was carrying. So, with a little bit of encouragement from myself, she decided to make an appointment with this well-known & highly-respected sports-injuries expert to see if he could free up the trapped nerve, or at least provide some kind of respite from her discomfort.

At about seven-thirty that same evening, the poor guy had phoned me. Nan was out at a coffee evening with her friends.

'It's not normal for me to discuss a patient's condition with their spouse, but I felt that I really had to speak to you about Nan,' he said nervously.

I froze in dread of what was coming next. I was right to do so.

'Mr McMurdo, your wife does not have a trapped nerve. I am almost certain that she has Multiple Sclerosis.'

So there I was, one hour later, sitting in my car with my big soulmate Cindy, and blubbering like a new-born baby. I had only ever witnessed one case of MS before, and that was my twenty-nine-year-old aunt who had died just two years later, leaving behind a heartbroken husband, a grief-stricken toddler son and a helpless six-month-old baby daughter. Right at that moment, I was absolutely frozen in fear of the future. I had been sobbing for at least half an hour by this time, and my normally very clinically-organised brain was totally frazzled and quite unable to think rationally.

It was around then that it dawned on me that Cindy had been sitting and staring at me the whole time. From the moment I had parked the car behind a row of small saplings at the river's edge, she hadn't moved a muscle. Not a bloody muscle.

I wiped my swollen eyes again on the sleeves of my shirt, and blew my nose into the dog's towel. I looked at my sorry face in the car's rear view mirror above the dashboard. My eyes were red and blotchy, and I remember thinking that I looked uncannily like one of the clowns in a travelling circus. Once again the horror of the situation struck home, and my stomach felt as if it had just been walloped by a heavyweight boxer's kidney punch. I threw open the driver's door and vomited. Very little came up, save for the last few vestiges of my own self-discipline.

My head was all over the place. Nan would be so devastated by this news that she would be totally unable to cope. She would be in a wheelchair by the time our baby was born, and the baby would have no mum by her second birthday.

My eyes completely filled up again, and I rested my head wearily on the steering wheel. To this day, I can still remember the constant 'drip-drip-drip' of my pathetic tears bouncing off the rubber floor mat at my feet.

And it was at that precise moment that the strangest thing happened, something that would change my outlook on life for ever.

As I extricated my weary head from the rim of the cheap plastic steering wheel and leaned back in the driver's seat, emotionally exhausted, I turned and looked at Cindy. She was still staring at me, completely motionless, apart from the steady rise and fall of her diaphragm, which moved in perfect synch with her gentle, rhythmic breathing. She was utterly and completely relaxed, totally at ease with life and not in the slightest bit perturbed at the sight of her lord-and-master making a complete dick of himself.

'Cindy, how can you be so bloody calm at a time like this?' I asked her wearily.

She blinked once and continued to gaze at me. Then her mouth, which had been closed up until that point, opened ever so slightly and I could just make out the tip of her tongue.

'You're smiling at me,' I said in an almost imperceptible whisper. Cindy tilted her head to one side and back again, continuing her gaze. Still, the very tip of her tongue just revealed itself, through her slightly-ajar mouth. I was convinced that she was smiling at me.

'I'm glad you're finding this funny,' I said to her.

At that, she drew in her tongue and closed her mouth. And in that instant, her face took on a much more serious expression. I realised immediately that she was not finding it funny at all, not one little bit.

'Cindy, just tell me that everything will work out fine. Please.'

Her ears rose and again her mouth opened slightly. Something else changed too. Something about her eyes.

'You're smiling again. You weren't laughing at all, were you lass? You were just smiling.'

Then the penny dropped. 'You're trying to talk to me, aren't you Cindy?' The slightest shiver ran up my spine.

Cindy held this expression and continued to stare at me, smiling or whatever it was she was really doing. No bored sighs, no impatient whines, no panting, no fidgeting, nothing. She was motionless, absolutely motionless, and she held my gaze like a hypnotist in the act of persuading an impressionable volunteer that he was actually a Hungarian donkey.

I stared back at Cindy and, for some reason, my own gaze was drawn towards her big brown eyes. I soon became completely mesmerised, and watched helplessly as her pupils seemed to dilate and contract, then dilate and contract again. And again, and again, and again.

I became lost in some parallel universe. My tears had gone, my fears had vanished along with them, and my breathing had slowed back to its normal rate, or perhaps even lower than normal. I was in a trance, completely lost in some fourth dimension, and I began to feel totally calm, totally at ease with the world.

I really don't know how long Cindy and I sat there, just gawking at each other. All I do know is that she was in charge of the situation, and she was communicating with me in some bizarre, but strangely reassuring way. She was talking to me. She was actually telling me things. Things I really needed to know.

Nan was very ill, but if we both gave her a lot of support, she would come through all of this. We would soon have a baby. The baby would be a little girl and she would be very, very special. There were really hard times around the corner, but I could 'lead us all' through these.

Finally, Cindy told me that it was very important for me to learn to speak with her, and that 'speaking' meant something very different from what I had understood it to mean.

'W-H-OOOOOOOO-S-H!'

I nearly jumped out of my skin. It was the tyres of a passing tractor whizzing through a puddle on the road behind us. I looked at my watch. It was half-past nine, and the daylight was beginning to fade.

'Oh shit!' I said aloud, as I realised that we had been sitting there for the best part of an hour, and that Nan was due home any minute now.

'What am I going to tell her, Cindy?' I asked in a bit of a panic.

At that point, the trance was well and truly broken. Cindy stretched, yawned and stood up, turning around once or twice and giving a few excited whimpers. Her tail began wagging furiously. She gave me first one paw, then the other, then both at once which she planked right on my weary shoulders and eyeballed me mischievously. A low, ear-piercing 'WOOF! WOOF!' split the silence and echoed around the car. We were back in the real world.

'Come on and we'll go for a wee walk, lass,' I said.

I opened the car door and out she bolted, straight into the shallow waters of the River Lugar where she picked up an enormous stick. I took it from her big soft mouth, heaved it downstream into a deeper pool, and she lunged gleefully after it.

Had I dreamt this whole thing, I wondered for a moment? As sure as hell, I hadn't dreamt the chiropractor's gut-wrenching diagnosis, that's for certain, as my stinging eyes would readily testify. But what about my 'discussion' with Cindy, in the car? Was that for real too, or simply a figment of my hyperactive imagination, fashioned out of intense psychological need?

No, it clearly hadn't been a dream, at least insofar as I had come to understand the meaning of the term, because I had remembered every single detail with crystal clarity. There had been no voices in our discussion, simply an uninterrupted two-way flow of weird but very vivid messages.

One stood out like a candle in the dark. I had to learn to 'speak' with Cindy, whatever that meant. I resolved there and then to begin my mission tomorrow. But for now, there was something else I had to do.

Somehow, I had to go home and tell my young wife that she had contracted Multiple Sclerosis, and would soon never walk again.

Learning To Speak With Our Mouths Shut

'An animal's eyes have the power to speak a great language.'
(Martin Buber, Existentialist Writer)

As I had promised Cindy in the car at Dalblair Bridge the previous snot-filled evening, I began my search the very next day for the key that I hoped would allow me to 'speak' with her. And so my search for the human-canine holy grail was well and truly under way. I also promised myself that if my mission were to prove successful, I would invite Doctor Dolittle and his assorted chums around for a game of poker and a few beers.

I decided to commence the process by doing a little bit of desktop research. I had no idea what I was actually looking for, not the slightest clue, but I just hoped that I would recognise it when I found it. One thing was clear though, and that was the fact that I badly needed this challenge, in order to absorb some cerebral thinking space that would otherwise have been totally exhausted by fretting twenty-four-seven about my poor young wife's increasingly desperate medical condition.

In the event, when she shuffled through the door after my return from the séance-in-the-country, I said nothing at all about the chiropractor's message of doom, having decided to keep it to myself for a few days at least. In a much needed spirit of pure defiance, I had managed to convince myself that if anyone was going to confirm the diagnosis-from-hell that would sentence Nan to a lifetime of chronic disability, it would be our own family doctor, not some bloody bone-cruncher whom I had never even met, and who should be sticking to the treatment of footballers' torn cruciate knee ligaments and elderly ladies' rickets.

That evening, I poured myself a generous whisky and sat back in my big armchair to reflect for a minute or two. It was very difficult indeed trying to focus on the subject matter, since time and again my deeply troubled mind kept wandering back to that scourge of young adults' lives, the one that rejoices in the name of Multiple Sclerosis. Somehow, however, I eventually managed to discipline myself to begin concentrating on the matter in hand, principally because of the sheer intensity I had seen in Cindy's eyes the night before, and the fact that her gaze had conveyed such an incredibly clear and coherent message to me.

My mind flashed back to the imaginary Meg, who had helped me to overcome so many fears in my early teens. Now I had a real live dog to guide me through the bad times that undoubtedly lay ahead. And how I needed a secret trusted soulmate.

'Okay, so what do we know already about the fascinating little world of communication, Mucky?' I asked myself.

I had acquired that particularly unappealing nickname when I was in first year at secondary school, on account of having been democratically elected as Lord Mucky, Great Chieftain of Clan Mucky, whose membership was the exclusive privilege of those in our cohort who happened to have a surname beginning with 'Mc' or 'Mac'. That had been my first taste of leadership, and I had risen to the occasion with a confidence, verve and megalomaniacal obsession that would prove to be absolute pre-requisite qualities for an aspiring big cheese.

So where should I begin? Well, I thought, I'm a trained school teacher after all, and I did actually attend the very occasional post-graduate lecture in teacher-pupil communication, now didn't I? At least, those at the end of each month when the attendance register was being circulated around the lecture theatre, I sniggered quietly to myself.

The fact was that I had worked like a galley slave for four years at University, and then swanned around like a penniless playboy whilst having to go through the relatively undemanding motions of post-graduate teacher training at college. My mate Willie and I had seriously considered taking out insurance policies to afford us some financial protection if, during that particular academic session, we were to be struck down with either cirrhosis of the liver or some horrible sexually transmitted disease. In the event we contracted neither, but I can assure you that it wasn't for the want of trying.

Okay then, could I muster up anything from my dim and not-too-distant college past that might possibly give me even the faintest bloody clue where to start?

Well, I did actually recall one particular piece of advice from college that had seemed to resonate and remain with me during my first two probationary years in the 'real' classroom. It fell somewhat short of rocket science, but took the form of one of our college lecturers saying that it's not what you say to your students in the classroom that matters, but it's the *panache* with which you say it that really makes all the difference to their understanding. What a complete dipstick, I had sniggered quietly to myself at the time, but for some strange reason that particular message had always stuck with me, and my early teaching experience had most certainly borne out his rather obvious, but immensely important advice.

So there was only one thing for it. Get the stepladder out of the garden shed and climb up into the attic. You see, I always had a propensity for lateral thinking.

There was, however, some degree of method in my madness, since lurking in the loft of our beloved semi-detached red sandstone villa, were my old college notes. Okay, I had copied most of these from my mates, having operated as we did at the time, a most ingenious 'rota system' to ensure group coverage of lectures, in order that we could take turns to test our intellectual skills more appropriately at the black jack table in the student beer bar. Furthermore, I had only read the blasted things once, the night before our end-of-session exam as I seem to recall which, incredibly, I actually managed to pass. It must have been a very difficult exam. And I don't think.

So off (and upwards) I went in pursuit of a big pile of dog-eared papers, which hitherto had held about as much fascination for me as a black-and-white compendium of Belgium's railway stations, but just on the off-chance that there might actually be a spark of genuine inspiration lurking amongst the cobwebs.

After a few minutes, I found my old notes in a rotting cardboard box, wedged between my redundant golf clubs and a home-brew beer kit that was bubbling away just nicely, thank you very much. I rummaged through the box and found the folder I was looking for. *'Effective Communication Skills'*, it read. What an original and inspiring title, I mused.

Rightly or wrongly, I had figured that if I wanted to make a semi-intelligent start on unlocking the mysteries of human-canine communication, then I might be well advised to begin by revisiting the principles that governed the interaction between human beings themselves. Thus, I set about taking my own notes from those I had previously scribbled down whilst completely zonked out of my wits by the monotonous drone of our bespectacled, bearded college lecturer, whose own communication skills could have passed as a commercial for mindless tedium itself. What a bloody bore he was.

Apparently, it all came down to the fact that the process of communication is predicated on at least two individuals sending and receiving a judicious mix of verbal signals (using words) and non-verbal signals (using anything except words). Again, hardly nuclear physics, but it was clearly going to be important to have that little principle imprinted firmly on my consciousness at all future times.

I wasn't particularly concerned about the verbal dimension, because I had already established that Cindy was bloody useless at articulating the English language, whereas I could do so quite effortlessly, save for the odd Friday evening, upon returning from the local pub with my so-called mates having led me astray once again. However, what I did find highly significant was the fact that, while Cindy was quite unable to verbalise human words, she could actually recognise a pretty decent number of these (about which more later).

Alternatively, it was the non-verbal communication dimension, or NVC as the boffins refer to it, that really fascinated me, because I knew with innate certainty that this was the communicative medium with which she had somehow managed to send me her very important 'messages'. So my further reading concentrated on the various components that make up the human NVC dimension, these including things like skeletal posture and body language, facial expressions and gestures, clothing and hairdos, and so on.

Oh yes, and something called eye contact too. Because it was this, or more accurately the face-to-face dimension of NVC with particular focus on eye-to-eye contact, that really intrigued me, since I was convinced – absolutely and utterly convinced – that it was this that Cindy had deployed the previous evening to deliver her canine messages of hope. Somehow I just instinctively knew that it was eye contact that held the key to 'speaking' with Cindy, as she had implored me to learn to do.

Now, I'll spare you the rather complex detail that I later unearthed in my subsequent study of both the verbal and non-verbal components of the process of human-canine communication, other than to say that I was becoming a good bit more enlightened about why the events of the previous evening might possibly have played out in the way they did.

Put in as crude a way as possible, this is what it all came down to.

Humans speak words
Dogs do not
Humans understand words
Dogs do too
Humans send non-verbal signals with their bodies, appendages and eyes
Dogs do too
Humans receive, process and interpret these non-verbal signals
Dogs do too

Therefore, to a significant degree at least, it had become clear to me that dogs are able to perform all of the same communicative tasks that humans claim to be able to perform. Except one, that is. Dogs are totally incapable of verbalising human words (although I do once remember a little dog appearing on a television programme one Friday evening, because his owner claimed to have taught him to say the word 'sausages', but it soon transpired to be bullshit rather than sausages).

Without any question of a doubt, Cindy, the ten-quid family pet, had conveyed some really important messages to me. Don't ask me how or why, and it certainly wasn't through the medium of the Queen's English, but somehow she had managed to tell me 'things'. My academic studies, my vocational training as a scientist, my professional work as a fledgling teacher, and my natural pragmatism and scepticism all conspired to tell me that all of this was just a right old load of complete claptrap, borne out of high emotions playing tricks on an over-sensitised mind at a time of great crisis.

However, I had been there, and 'it' had actually happened. Cindy had spoken to me with her body, and with her face, and with her eyes. She had given me vital information that I could never have received otherwise. Yes, she had told me things I desperately wanted to hear, but these were things I needed to know for purely practical reasons too.

What really gripped my attention, though, was the inter-relationship between facial expression and eye contact in the communication process, because I was absolutely convinced that Cindy had 'spoken' to me principally with her face and her eyes. And before the agnostics among you all jump to the otherwise laudable conclusion that I have completely taken leave of my senses, please allow me to paraphrase just one extract from Charles Darwin's *The Expression of the Emotions in Man and Animals* (1872), in which he made an extremely important statement that really gripped me by the proverbial short-and-curlies, and that was this. All mammals show emotion readily in their faces.

So there you go, if you don't buy any of this highly imaginative stuff, try arguing with Darwin and see where that gets you. Your move, pal.

Quite simply, I knew with innate certainty that Cindy had been 'smiling' at me the previous evening, trying with all her heart to convince and reassure me that everything would work out, and that all would be fine and dandy.

And then, just as I was reflecting on the few crumbs of wisdom that I had picked up in the last couple of hours, for some reason I allowed my still-troubled mind to drift back in time again to the chiropractor's verbal uppercut with which he had knocked me out for the mandatory eight-count. However, I had now begun staggering back to my feet, and I was gradually regaining consciousness, thanks to an ever-so-slightly heightened theoretical understanding of human-canine communication, accentuated exponentially by a few non-verbal messages from a behaviourally-challenged dog.

I was getting my act together again. Mucky was back.

Okay, so where had this little wealth of rather quaint information left me? Well, the previous evening, I had most definitely been in a state of ultra-high cognitive and emotional perception, that's for sure. Put another way, my cerebral activity levels were running riot and my imagination was galloping out of control. However, the one thing that I had noticed above all else about Cindy's body language, facial expression and eye contact was the frequency, indeed the bewildering rapidity, of dilatory changes in her pupils.

Was it by some strange combination of her superbly controlled body posture, her reassuring facial 'smile', and her involuntary yet amazingly well-developed eye contact and pupil dilation patterns that she had been conveying to me a blindingly clear message?

Whatever the physical or metaphysical mechanics involved, that message was this. There was now a very bright light at the end of the hitherto dark tunnel down which I had been staring like a terrified child.

Cindy had spoken to me without saying a word. Not a single word. How I wished that we could all learn to speak with our big mouths shut.

The world might just be a better place for it.

The Art Of Intellectual Disobedience

'Anybody who doesn't know what soap tastes like, never washed a dog.'
(Franklin P. Jones, Author)

Paradoxically, since our communal trance in the car and in the light of my early research, I was now beginning to see Cindy in a whole new light. Up until that point, I had only ever thought of our first canine acquisition as a bright-eyed, bushy-tailed, happy and adorable bloody nutcase.

Nan and I had purchased a book, rather imaginatively entitled *'Training Your Puppy'*, and three times we had each read the damned thing from cover to cover but, in truth, it had made very little difference. We had already worked out that Cindy was a very intelligent young dog, quick to recognise numerous words and react to various stimuli, but most unwilling to conform to those commands which she deemed in any way to be unappealing to her.

Into the bargain, the fact that neither of us had any experience whatsoever of owning or training a dog loomed very large in the proceedings. In short, Cindy was as sharp as a tack, but determined to do things her way, while we had great intentions of rearing a well-schooled puppy, but not the foggiest idea how to implement our master plan.

Quite simply, Cindy hadn't read the book.

Perhaps we had tried to teach her too many different verbal commands at the one time. There again, perhaps we just simply didn't have a clue. Who knows? Two things were fairly certain, though. Firstly, Cindy clearly understood what it was that we were asking her to do and, secondly, she was damned if she was going to be doing it, unless it was right up her alley.

Our quaint little puppy manual had advised us that training puppy should be 'fun', and it certainly turned out to be just that. For Cindy, that is.

I actually kept a hand-written journal of our training sessions, as advised by the book's author, an Armenian-born former ballet dancer who now lived on a cattle farm in southern Texas. With such a traditional canine background as that, how could we possibly fail?

The training sessions, a gross misnomer if ever there was one, had taken place in various locations, the more basic ones in the house or in the back garden, whilst the more adventurous lessons involved trips in the car to assorted and mercifully secluded spots in the country.

At the conclusion of each session, Cindy would inevitably be found cavorting around in manic euphoria and barking herself silly, having enjoyed half an hour of absolute mayhem, mischievous disobedience and copious dog-biscuit consumption, in reward for her rather lovable truculence. Meanwhile, yours truly would be in urgent need of a wee lie-down in a darkened room to bring his galloping stress levels back down to survivable proportions. It really was that bad at times.

Allow me, if you will, to paraphrase some of the hopelessly naive instructions from our puppy-training book, together with a brief account of Cindy's progress towards their stated objectives. For ease of contextualisation, I will present these command-at-a-time, and in the order we tried them out on Cindy.

Our ballerina-cum-milkmaid's theory was that every time we gave a certain verbal command, and then backed it up with the associated hand signal, the message would be delivered subliminally, reinforced through practice, and the response would improve incrementally until, after a fairly brief period of time, the command would be well and truly learned, completely embedded and inextricably internalised within the puppy's behavioural pattern for eternity, or even longer if you practised hard enough.

A laudable enough theory, don't you think? Well, how would you like to hear about the reality?

Okay, then, here goes. Incidentally, the fictitious dog in the training manual was supposed to have been a four-month-old Springer Spaniel called Becky, which is of course one of the commonest girls' names in all Armenia.

First Command: 'Sit!'
'Drop your arm by your side, then bend your elbow and raise your hand above Becky's head, and give the command. Within a very short time, Becky will learn to sit still. At first, she will probably try to stand up again within a few seconds, but keep repeating the procedure over and over, and she will soon learn that she only gets her reward when she stays put.'

Cindy's Actual Response:
It took us a mere two minutes to teach Cindy to sit, but try as we might, we couldn't get her to keep her backside on the ground for more than two seconds at a time, neither for love nor money nor dog biscuits dipped in Bisto gravy. She was clearly informing us that she knew fine well what we wanted her to do, and that on the promise of a biscuit she was quite prepared to do it, however transiently, but on immediate receipt of which she had absolutely no intention of prolonging the learned obedience for another nanosecond.

Second Command: 'Stay!'
'Stretch your hand outwards from your shoulder and in Becky's direction, then give the verbal command. At first, she will want to come with you wherever you try to go, but you must keep repeating the command and only give Becky her reward when she stays where you have decided to seat her. This could well take a bit of time and hard work, but practice makes perfect.'

<u>Cindy's Actual Response:</u>

I seem to remember that we attempted to justify our abject failure in getting Cindy to perform this basic task, on our rather quaint belief that Labradors were much too inquisitive and energetic to sit on their backsides simply doing nothing for any length of time. Eventually we just gave up the ghost, because the whole procedure would eventually have rendered me insane, and Nan in unnecessarily prolonged agony from quite helpless laughter at my sorry expense. Cindy would go on to achieve many things in life, but sitting on her arse for any length of time was never, ever going to be one of them.

Third Command: 'Come Here!'

'Point straight at Becky with your arm outstretched, and bend it back until your forefinger is pointing towards your own face, then give the verbal command. This is one of the easiest commands for Becky to understand, since she will already be minded to come to you for two reasons. Firstly, she will instinctively want to be reunited with you anyway, and secondly she will be attracted by your exciting arm-bending motion.'

<u>Cindy's Actual Response:</u>

This one actually did work pretty successfully in the house. Every time I said 'Come Here!' Cindy would bolt to my side in search of her dog biscuit. However, attempting the same command in the back garden was a completely different story, in that all it actually managed to achieve was to send her off in the diametrically opposite direction towards the blackcurrant bushes in search of her lost toy, which was clearly a much more attractive proposition than a pat on the head from her alleged master.

Fourth Command: 'Side!'

'Slap your right buttock with your right hand and gently pull Becky's lead so that she comes round your back from your left side to your right side, then give the vocal command. (There are

various theories about this, but I prefer my dogs to walk to my right, since I am right-handed.) At first, Becky will find it difficult to understand what you actually want her to do. She will probably start tugging backwards on her lead, and resist or stop in her tracks altogether. However, you must never pull sharply or drag her. Instead, just stop and restart the whole procedure, again and again, until the message is learned and fully reinforced. This activity may be a bit frustrating at first, for both Becky and yourself, but again practice makes perfect.'

Cindy's Actual Response:
Frustrating? You don't say? Nan and I were simply convinced that Labradors had been designed not to concern themselves in the slightest about where they were supposed to be going, but just to get there as quickly as possible, and certainly before anyone else did. Every Saturday morning, my neighbours would greet me with 'Good morning Ian, I see Cindy's taking you for a walk again?', as she hauled me near-horizontally along the pavement. By the time I returned home, the knees would invariably be out of my trousers and my right arm would be so distended that I could have scratched the soles of my feet without bending my legs.

Fifth Command: 'Get Down!'
'To prevent Becky from jumping up on you, or worse still on an innocent pedestrian, just say 'Get Down!' and immediately turn your back on her. She will soon begin to fret that you are ignoring her, and then get the message that she must not jump up on people. Becky will be desperate for attention, hence the reason she will at first want to jump up on you, on members of your family and probably on passers-by too. However, she will hate it when you turn your back on her and ignore her, since that will make her feel unwanted. If you keep practising, she will soon stop this extremely annoying and sometimes dangerous activity.'

<u>Cindy's Actual Response:</u>
Cindy was simply a nightmare in this regard. She seemed absolutely driven to stand or jump on her hind legs whenever someone appeared over the horizon, be it friend or foe. Eyeballing them at face level seemed to be her main driving force, frequently coupling that activity with licking their assorted faces from chin to crown. All the 'ignoring' routine really achieved was to make her even more determined to get her various subjects' attention by leaping even more manically upon the poor souls. Indeed, if they continued ignoring her, she would then start scratching their clothes until she eventually had their completely undivided attention. Elderly dog-phobic ladies wearing luminous pink trousers appeared to be Cindy's particular favourites, especially after she had been rolling in a mud-filled ditch (which was almost always, really). I simply lost count of the number of times she knocked me over while I was bending down to tie my shoe laces, and she once famously knocked the local minister's spectacles right off his serious little face, converting them into a ten-piece jigsaw puzzle on the kitchen floor, as the dreary old soul attempted to console Nan on the death of her father.

Sixth Command: 'Fetch! / Dead!'
'Ask Becky to sit and stay, while you throw your object of choice away. Immediately upon the vocal command of 'Fetch! point in the direction of the thrown object. Only reward her when she brings the object back to you, and once more when she drops the object upon your vocal command of 'Dead!' Becky's natural inclination will at first be to bolt after the thrown object immediately, but you must insist on her staying put until you give the 'Fetch!' command. This may well take a bit of time and practice. Likewise, when she retrieves the object, she will initially be reluctant to drop it from her mouth. However, perseverance and timely reward will eventually prevail.'

<u>Cindy's Actual Response:</u>
Oh, so you bloody think so? The Cossack ballerina should have tried throwing a stick with Cindy anywhere in the neighbourhood. She would have been counting her fingers in the aftermath, and finding great difficulty in getting past three. Persuading Cindy to sit and stay was difficult enough, but when I had a ball or a toy in my hand it was damned-near impossible. The very moment I picked something up, there was no way on earth that her bottom could conceivably maintain any form of contact with the ground. No siree, not a hope. Onto the next unsuccessful trick.

Seventh Command: 'Speak! / Shush!'
'With Becky sitting facing you, hold out one of her favourite treats and ask her to 'Speak!' This is one of the really easy commands to teach her, since before long she will simply bark out of frustration. Whenever she does, you have to reward her immediately. Once this has been fully mastered, try the opposite command of 'Shush!' At first, Becky might try all sorts of other diversionary tactics to get her reward, such as jumping up on you or giving you a paw, but you really must resist all these antics. Eventually she will become frustrated and completely unable to resist barking, at which point you must reward her immediately. She will therefore quickly learn that your 'Speak!' command means that she should bark at once. The same routine can then be established for the opposite command of 'Shush!"

<u>Cindy's Actual Response:</u>
What? Have you ever tried getting your first-ever Labrador pup to shut up when you've got a dog biscuit in your hand? It's like asking a two-month-old Malaysian baby to recite Tam O' Shanter in fluent Swahili. The actual 'speaking' thing was no bother at all to Cindy, since she would have quoted an entire soliloquy from William Shakespeare for a dog chew, but getting her to button it was another thing entirely. It's very important to make your dog bark on command, for example when a stranger

appears at the door, but if you seriously believe that you can ask a Labrador to stop barking when another dog is in your garden, or when the neighbour's cat is sitting grinning on the window ledge, then I want a pint of whatever you're drinking.

The training book's highly dubious advice didn't end there, oh no. There were about fifty of the blasted things and you would have needed a dog with a *Mensa*-compatible IQ to have even the remotest chance of getting the poor thing to understand even half of them, let alone build them into its daily routine. Fortunately, I had a dog with the pre-requisite smarts, but unfortunately one who also had an amazing determination to do things her way, or not at all. Nan and I had a term for Cindy's philosophy on life, which suited her just fine. We called it 'intellectual disobedience'.

Some of the puppy instruction manual's intended commands were even more fanciful. One was intended to teach your dog to *'Eat!'* which the book's fetchingly quaint blurb described thus. *'Point your forefinger straight ahead at Becky's food dish, and say "Eat!"'.* In Cindy's case, or indeed with any Labrador Retriever I've ever met, the food in the dish would already be making its way into the small intestine by the time your finger had reached the horizontal position. Quite simply, Labradors would eat anything and everything, their owners included if they sat in a stationary position for long enough. In fact, one day when Cindy was only six months old, we lost her somewhere in the house. We searched every single room, our big fitted wardrobes, under the beds and everywhere we could think of. About half an hour later, I found her completely comatose inside her puppy food bag, with a hugely distended belly. She had eaten herself to sleep.

And then, it came to pass that, one evening, the inevitable happened. After returning utterly worn out from yet another dreadfully dispiriting sojourn-in-the-country with our training manual, I sat down, poured Nan and myself a glass of wine, gave Cindy yet another dog chew, and switched on the television. The very moment that my weary backside crash-landed in sheer exhaustion onto my favourite armchair, the little bastard ran out of the living room with the remote control in her mouth, then bolted up the stairs, no doubt to hide it under the bed.

I sipped my wine ruefully, then heaved my badly-chewed copy of *Training Your Puppy* into the dustbin.

Down By The Seaside

'Disobedience, the rarest and most courageous of the virtues, is seldom
distinguished from neglect, the laziest and commonest of the vices.'
(George Bernard Shaw, author and playwright)

If there was one day that was to epitomise Cindy's whole
approach to life, then it must surely have been the fourth of July,
1975.

Independence Day, I hear you say. Well yes, Cindy's personal
independence day, actually. A day that would go down in
folklore as that on which the most innocent-looking big dog
imaginable contrived to scale the heights of the most
unimaginable mischievousness, eventually stopping just a few
millimetres short of complete anarchy. It really was quite
unbelievable to behold.

So there all three of us were, bright-eyed and bushy-tailed on
that glorious sun-kissed summer's morning, having just watched
the toffee-nosed little brat of a weather girl on national television
offering her heart-warming forecast of wall-to-wall sunshine
and scorching temperatures, the latter expected to reach the
high seventies or even the low eighties by mid-afternoon. Bring
it on!

Thus, having scoffed our respective breakfasts far too quickly
– toast and jam for the human beings, and a tin of the most
hideously foul-smelling dog food for the manic mutt – we began
excitedly to prepare the essentials for our trip to the beach on
our native Ayrshire coast. As we concocted a rather confused
assortment of gammon, tomato, cheese and boiled egg
sandwiches, topped up the vacuum flask with milky coffee and
retrieved a selection of barely-used sun tan lotions from cold
storage, an aura of scarcely-concealed glee hung in the air. I

could almost smell it. Unfortunately, so too could the one with the floppy ears, beaming bright eyes and ever-swishing tail.

When I think back to the sheer exhilaration of that July morning all those years ago, I remember many things with fond affection, but two in particular. Firstly, I will never forget the air of happiness and excitement that enveloped our precious home that day, and after I had powdered my proverbial nose prior to departure, the slightest tear that I shed whilst looking into the bathroom mirror and thanking the good lord silently for the wonderful little family with which he had blessed me. Secondly, neither will I ever forget Cindy's body language that day, nor more specifically the look in her eyes. The latter was one of brain-bursting anticipation and crazed hyper-excitement, and defined the psyche of a young dog fit to explode in a hopelessly forlorn effort to contain herself. I really ought to have known better than unleash her onto an unsuspecting beach in a state like that.

Preparations complete, I began packing the car. First of all I grabbed the picnic, all of which had been very caringly arranged by Nan herself in the empty wicker basket that we had previously been given as a once-bulging Christmas hamper, and deposited it in the boot of the car, accompanied by the other obligatory accoutrements such as plastic cutlery, paper napkins and the like. Then it was Cindy's turn to be deposited into the back seat, red lead attached to her brown leather collar as usual.

Finally, I ushered Nan from the big oak door of our house up the front path to the wrought-iron gate, her right hand grasping a walking stick in a vice-like grip, while her left grabbed my own right forearm as if her very life depended on it.

By that stage, the whole process of getting Nan from the relative security of our home to the passenger's seat of the car normally took about fifteen minutes all-in, but we were beginning to get used to such protracted procedures by then. We would certainly have to, because these were the cards of life with which my young wife had been dealt, and she now had no alternative but to play them for the rest of her mortal existence.

Other than quitting the game altogether, of course, but Nan was much too bloody tough to throw in the towel as easily as that. However, as she often reminded me at the time, she had one big person and one little 'person' right by her side to support her, the former still sporting his by now seriously out-of-fashion Beatle haircut, and the latter in the form of a certain canine companion who had been God-sent to us to convert every single dark moment into gales of howling laughter.

Despite our setbacks, we were the happiest family on planet earth, no doubt about it. Little did I realise that, in only a few years' time, our joy would actually contrive to blossom even more exponentially, on entrance to this world of the two wonderful children that we once thought we would never be able to have, but whom the manic mutt in the back seat would soon protect against all harm.

About forty-five minutes later, we had reached 'The Electric Brae', a rather curious phenomenon which is really just a simple stretch of tarmac road a few miles south of the seaside town of Ayr, that boasts a rather uncanny power, which is this. If you stop your car on the brae and leave its gear in neutral, it will soon start rolling up the hill. No kidding. Don't ask me how it happens, but it just does. You really ought to give it a try sometime, but best not to let your insurance company know, lest some ten-ton lorry laden with Ayrshire potatoes should come ploughing into your rear bumper while you are playing this quaint but rather silly little game. Anyway, I digress as usual.

A few hundred metres further on, our right indicator light began flashing and we were soon on our precarious way down the steep road that leads to Croy Shore, three sets of teeth chattering as our wheels bumped over every single undulation on what in those days was little more than a badly-potholed dirt track road. We arrived at the foot of the hill and turned left, to behold the magnificent golden sands of Croy shore that stretch for mile-upon-mile, until they ultimately meet with the rising banks that lead up to the resplendent grounds of the famous Culzean Castle.

Like the dozens of similarly energised families who had already arrived there even earlier than we had done, we drove along the beach until we found a lovely spot beside our own chosen sand dune, parked the car and unloaded all its human, canine and inanimate contents. Ten minutes later, I had managed to manoeuvre Nan's backside onto a big travelling rug on the sand, and Cindy was absolutely nowhere to be seen. Gone.

'CINDY!' I bellowed. Nothing.

'CINDY!' Still nothing.

'Where the bloody hell is she?' I muttered to myself, in one of my infamous stage whispers that everyone within a six-mile radius can normally hear.

I surveyed the scene and considered the possibilities. There were about fifty-one of them by my reckoning, these being any one of the half-century of families currently unpacking their respective lunches, and the fifty-first itself, which was anywhere at all in the big pond that calls itself the Atlantic Ocean.

After at least ten minutes of increasing frustration, my hollering eventually bore fruit, as I spied a big golden-yellow dog galloping towards me at tremendous velocity.

'COME ON CINDY!' I shouted, and she sprinted faster and faster, closer and closer.

'Nan, what ……….. what's that she's got in her mouth?' I asked rather hesitantly. 'Is it a plastic bag ……….. or a football ………… or a big toy or something? And it's sort of shining too?'

It was then that I also saw a hefty, rather bad-tempered-looking, bald-headed man attempting to run after her, in utterly forlorn chase.

'Oh my God!' said Nan, in evidence of her own perfect twenty-twenty vision, which still to this day surpasses my own by approximately nineteen-nineteen. 'Ian, it's a bloody chicken! It's a whole chicken in a bit of tinfoil!'

And a whole chicken it most certainly was. Cindy had clearly nicked it from God-alone-knows whom or where, although it began very quickly to dawn on me that it might have had something to do with the thankfully out-of-shape big guy who was giving pathetic chase in his shorts and flip-flops, gasping for air and sweating profusely by the time he was nearing our vicinity.

Alas, by the time I had given the 'DEAD!' command to Cindy (courtesy of a few words of wisdom from the aforementioned acrobatic Armenian cowgirl), the poor guy's lunch was half-eaten and the remnants were covered in sand and seaweed.

Once I had calmed the poor man down, and bribed him a fiver to seek alternative lunch supplies for his starving family, who were waiting in quiet anticipation at the other end of the beach, thus preventing him from inflicting any acts of heinous violence on my own, I shoved Cindy's red lead over her neck and took her for a little walk.

'You need to calm down, Cindy, or I'm putting you on the next bus to Cumnock,' I scolded her rather insincerely, as I sat her down in the adjacent meadow to let her get her breath back.

Her perfectly erect body posture, swishing tail and grinning visage seemed to reply with a defiant, yet engagingly innocent, 'Oh no you won't, because you love me too much!'

More than anything else, I still recall the sheer fun and mischief that just seemed to burst from her big bright eyes. The truth was that the more outrageously naughty Cindy's behaviour transpired to be, the more unavoidably hilarious I would find the whole situation, so hopelessly immature and recklessly carefree was I in those days.

When I think back to the innocence of the times, and contrast my canine pack leadership determination nowadays to its breathtaking absence 'way back then, I always laugh out loud. However, as my own two dogs stroll somewhat more obediently by my side these days, I often wonder if Cindy's everlasting ethereal presence in our home has ever spilled the beans on the relatively liberal regime in which she, herself, once ruled supreme.

Episode 1 (10.30), or 'the chicken-in-tinfoil incident', as it would more infamously transpire to be dubbed for posterity, was to herald the first of an amazing catalogue of outrageous incidents of comparable mischievousness that particular day. And all of this despite our completely redundant discussion in the meadow, as a result of which my influence on Cindy's behaviour had clearly fallen somewhat short of overwhelming. This is how the remainder of our day at the seaside played out.

Episode 2 (11.15)
Cindy decides to visit the family located at the adjacent sand dune, comprising a small skinny man and his huge rotund wife (it would have been fascinating to see some polaroid photographs of their romantic get-togethers, but only from a purely practical physics point of view, you understand). Beside them on the sand lie their two teenage daughters, who look completely bored out of their skulls, and a three-legged Jack Russell terrier with one-and-a-half ears, which Cindy has clearly worked out will pose no threat, most probably on account of her own numerical superiority from a physical appendage standpoint. How wrong can she be? The very moment she introduces herself by sniffing at its backside, the cross little bastard turns on her and she immediately bolts from whence she came and perches her backside right on my bare chest as I lie contentedly baking in the sun's morning rays. I am left for the remainder of that summer with five huge scratches that run from my shoulders to my belly button.

Episode 3 (12.05)
Having been sprawled out, slow-roasting in the sun for well over an hour by now, albeit hardly relaxing on account of the requirement to be extremely vigilant about Cindy's assorted antics, I decide to take her a walk down to the sea, both of us then paddling and splashing happily in the gentle, lapping waves. I find a huge stick and throw it out into the sea, with Cindy in hot pursuit as always, and we play like this for ages,

while my poor Nan can only sit and wave to us from the security of her travelling rug. How she would have loved to be paddling along beside us, I remember thinking ruefully. After a good half-hour or so, we wander back to base, but not before Cindy has introduced herself to a family who have begun unwrapping their sausage rolls and tuna sandwiches, and then deposits the biggest canine turd ever witnessed by mankind, right in front of the dear old granny, who must have been ninety-five if she was a day. The horror on their faces as I pick up the nauseating deposit in a paper hankie will live with me forever. 'Ian, your face is sunburnt already,' opines Nan as I walk towards her. 'No, it isn't,' I reply. 'That's not sunburn, it's pure humiliation.' When I tell her the story, she nearly chokes in a fit of hysterics.

Episode 4 (13.45)
'That wee lad will never get his kite to fly on a calm day like this. There's hardly a breath of air. What's his old man thinking about?' I laugh out loud, as the latter sprints effeminately across the sand in a pathetically futile effort to get the thing airborne. After about fifteen minutes of abject failure, he gives up the ghost. However, the wee boy, clearly disillusioned by his dad's hopeless failure, then picks up the ball of string himself and runs across the sand towards the sea as fast as his little legs will propel him. I think it was probably his shout of, 'LOOK AT ME, DADDY!' that attracts Cindy's attention, and off she storms in hot pursuit. 'NO, CINDY! NO!' I bellow to a pair of temporarily deaf ears. Within a matter of seconds, she pounces upon the paper kite that is bouncing impotently along the sand, unintentionally ripping the string out of the young lad's hands and causing him to perform the most spectacular reverse summersault I have ever witnessed - and that even includes some pretty decent efforts by a whole host of skeletal Russian gymnasts. The wee boy howls in a hybrid of pain and embarrassment, while I smack Cindy on the arse, and then have to go and grovel apologetically to his parents. 'For God's sake Cindy!' I yell at her. 'When are you going to behave?' She smacks

her lips, but forgets to stop wagging her tail. Her eyes twinkle in the sunshine, and I end up splitting my sides yet again.

Episode 5 (14.40)
By this time, all eyes on Croy shore seem to be staring in our direction, even those peering either side of the ferocious beaks adorning the big confident heads of the enormous seagulls who are circling the picnickers in search of some titbits to augment their already substantial seafood intake. And make no mistake about it, Cindy is the focal point of everyone's attention. However, she has still to perform her *finale*, her *encore* if you will. As we all sit on the travelling rug, having partaken of our own sandwiches and attempting to recuperate from the day's mayhem, Cindy now finds herself manacled by a rope to the car's exhaust pipe, to prevent any further such acts of canine terrorism (which is exactly where she should have been put in the first place, I suppose). As we begin to pack up again, having by then had quite enough exposure to the sun's UV rays and Cindy's repertoire of mischievous misdeeds, I untie her temporarily in order to put her back in the car. However, in that very instant - that mere split nanosecond of freedom - she has spied something rather more interesting on the horizon. It is a five-a-side football match on the beach. So off she hares again, straight into the thick of it, and grabs the footballers' beach ball between her teeth and her claws. As I sprint over to rescue the proceedings, I again shout, 'NO, CINDY! NO!' The next sound I hear is a kind of 'P-P-S-S-S-S-S-S-S-H-H', and the beach ball begins to disintegrate like a cheese *soufflé* gone wrong. Game over. As ten similarly deflated would-be soccer players glare at us in furious dismay, I plop Cindy's lead over her neck and hotfoot it back to base. 'Time to go home,' I say ruefully to Nan, who by this time is perilously close to wetting herself in laughter.

'Cindy, how do you think you behaved today?' I asked her after she had eaten her dinner and slumped wearily into her bed in the kitchen.

'Pretty well, I think,' her eyes seemed to say in reply.

'Considering all the distractions you put in front of me,' she added.

I laughed aloud, kissed her mighty forehead and stood back to look at her, as she curled up into an innocent ball of golden fur. Her eyes gradually became heavy with the day's exertions, but not before they had radiated a final message to her alleged master.

'Now, if you really don't mind, I could do with a wee bit of kip now. I need to recharge up my batteries for tomorrow, you know.'

Conversational Dogmanese

'No one appreciates the very special genius of your conversation as your dog does.'
(Christopher Morley, Author and Journalist)

Now you might be forgiven for thinking that someone who would contrive in later life to hold down public office, may have had his thinking influenced by the great philosophers of our illustrious past, such as Aristotle and Plato, and then further moulded into shape by more contemporary leadership gurus like Fullan and Covey. Well, despite the undoubted talents that these highly respected individuals undoubtedly possess, I'm afraid you'd be quite wrong, because my own particular role models all tended to be drawn from the great cartoon characters of my formative years, many of whom were of non-human form into the bargain.

Please find, below, my assorted superheroes, alongside the associated qualities for which I so admired them:

Bugs Bunny	Resourcefulness
Popeye The Sailor Man	Admirable protectiveness of ugly spouse
Road Runner	Devastating acceleration from 0 – 60 mph
Wile E. Coyote	Indefatigability
Jessica Rabbit	Magnificent bosom
Jerry Mouse	Courage under intense intimidation
Sylvester	Valiant attempts to exterminate irritating canary
Yogi Bear	Perseverance (and humility)
Fred Flintstone	Inventiveness (in the face of low tolerance level)
Penelope Pitstop	Tremendous legs
Dick Dastardly	Blind ambition
Tasmanian Devil	Incredible centrifugal force

Even by that stage, man's best friend seemed to loom large in the much-needed development of my emotional intelligence, often but sadly not always in an inspirational sense.

For example, in the fifties and sixties, *Lassie*, a rather scruffy big Shetland Collie, was all the rage. Now I fully appreciate that *Lassie* wasn't a cartoon character *per se*, but as far as I was concerned she may as well have been, because she seemed to be impervious to every conceivable mortal danger and completely dissociated from the laws of physics. To put it another way, *Lassie* was simply not a credible character, at least not to me.

Deputy Dawg was another imposter, if you ask me. And not just because of the fact that a hound had been appointed by the local townsfolk as their deputy sheriff – and in a democratic election, if you please - but on account of the fact that he was semi-articulate into the bargain (with the emphasis very much on 'semi'). After all, I had always thought that, 'way back then, mid-western cops couldn't have strung three consecutive words together to save their lives.

So therein lay my dilemma. Having had my adolescent thinking moulded by such disarming propaganda about surreal animal caricatures and canine imposters, and further influenced by my very recent personal experience with Cindy and associated desktop research, I was now well and truly off on a mission to develop our very own human-canine hybrid language.

I was absolutely convinced that there had been a steadily increasing two-way flow of information between Cindy and me over the past few weeks and, as a trained and hitherto sceptical scientist, I simply had to find a rational explanation for this, in order to sustain my much-needed faith that I had now at last found my secret trusted soulmate. And no longer one whose ethereal presence I had to convince myself was lying metaphysically on my bed, but one whose glorious and very substantial physical presence was firmly welded to my side in my time of great need. In effect, Cindy and I were beginning to develop an uncanny ability to 'connect' with each other.

It was around then that I decided to call our language *Dogmanese*. Politically correct it was not but, sadly, that black art had still not managed to dominate my thinking. Thus, having established a proper name for our language, the only other thing that I hadn't yet completely figured out was precisely how it would all eventually come together. A mere detail, I told myself encouragingly.

However, from my embryonic research, I now knew one thing for sure. Whatever *Dogmanese* might ultimately turn out to be, it would certainly not be an exclusively 'spoken' language, as you or I might define such a thing. *Dogmanese* would not be composed merely of words – although words obviously did play a part for much of the time – and therefore it would inevitably be much less indigenous, parochial and culturally-dependent than the multitudinous 'national' languages that have been developing on the planet since the dawn of time. In other words (if you will pardon the rather cheap pun), and given the fact that *Dogmanese* would necessarily be heavily dependent on various non-spoken components, it clearly had the potential to be much more 'international' than that, a thought that really excited me.

So I decided to spend the next few days looking a lot more closely at the dynamics involved when Cindy and I were 'on message', and see what they actually looked like. And all of this aided and abetted by my copious research literature, of course, in order to prevent me straying down the occasional blind and very misleading alley.

I had already established that Cindy had managed successfully to communicate with me, with members of my family and indeed with other dogs, in a whole variety of ways. First of all, and although she wasn't a particularly noisy dog as such, she seemed to place a fair bit of emphasis on communicating by sound, whether that was by means of her deep booming bark, her attention-seeking whimper, her disapproving grumble, or whatever. The way she held her body, and especially her head, conveyed to me some pretty clear signals about her mood and spirits. Her ears and her tail frequently radiated some rather obvious messages to me.

However, without a shadow of a doubt it was her face that brought these messages to life, and particularly her eyes. They really could tell a thousand tales, and some of these in considerable detail as well, as I had already discovered very recently to dramatic effect.

Some of the communicative techniques that Cindy deployed were so basic that a two-year-old child could have interpreted the messages she was attempting to send. For example, when it was nearing her dinner time, she would just stare and stare and stare, alternating the direction of her gaze every few seconds between my own eyes and the hall cupboard door, immediately behind which her food lay in waiting. Then immediately after she had been fed, she would run over to her cardboard box and bring me a toy, to inform me that it was now 'playtime'. If she was getting bored, and thought that it was high time I took her out for a walk, Cindy would have no hesitation in bringing her leash straight over to me, and plopping it down at my feet, then eyeballing me for as long as it took to get me up off my lazy backside.

The range of techniques that Cindy used was enormous. I always found that she was at her happiest and most content when she had succeeded in conveying to me some important message or other, whether that took the form of her dropping her empty water dish on the floor and then finding that I would immediately fill it up, or something more spiritual like sending me an intense signal with her eyes and then realising that I had interpreted the subliminal message it contained.

Now, all of this might seem a wee bit strange and even quite challenging to those of you who have never actually owned a pet, but believe me, effective communication is every bit as important for animals' psychological security as it is for our own. Indeed, when you consider that certain animals, including dogs, are completely incapable of articulating any human words at all, and yet really adept at recognising and understanding quite a number of them, then it is hardly surprising that they have had to develop numerous other means of communicating meaningfully with each other, and with the *Homo Sapiens* in their lives.

The fact of the matter is, of course, that human beings can carry out a number of very useful tasks that dogs just can't even attempt to replicate, simply because we can do one thing that they are quite unable to even contemplate. We can stand up straight on our 'hind legs', and they cannot. It is that which enables us to leave our 'front legs' (or arms, as I prefer to call them) free to perform a whole host of impressive actions. We can carry briefcases and handbags. We can rotate a car steering wheel with one hand while changing gear with the other (I actually used to be able to eat a bacon sandwich and dictate a letter at the same time too, but I'm damned if I can remember how I managed it all at the same time). We can write out our shopping lists, type on our keyboards, tile the bathroom wall and knit woolly sweaters. We can play the guitar, or perhaps even the grand piano, or if we feel like really annoying the neighbours, we can wallop a big set of drums for hours on end in the pitch black of the morning. We can wave our arms around manically and gesticulate to others, thereby augmenting our already very well-refined verbal communication skills still further. We can brush our teeth, pick our noses and scratch our arses, although it is always best to remember to do so in that particular order of chronology.

Sadly, however, the poor dog just can't compete in terms of the 'front legs' dimension, because it simply does not enjoy the luxury of using these for such social and communicative purposes. Alternatively, the dog requires them to stay in contact with the ground for most of the time, leaving only its mouth with which to attempt all those other interesting things that we do with our arms and hands. It really is a dog's life, when you come to think about it.

On the other hand (another hopelessly pathetic pun, and I really must learn to stop this nonsense), Cindy's word recognition capacity was absolutely amazing, even if she couldn't articulate a single syllable. In fact, we had a couple of good friends called Kevin and Eileen who had a baby girl of about eighteen-months-old at the time, and I remember being completely convinced that Cindy could actually recognise a lot more words than little Eva herself had clocked by then. Having said that, the bright little creature had already learned to utter at least a dozen 'Da-Das', 'Pee-Pees', 'Din-Dins' and the like, while my poor Cindy just sat there in frustrated silence, waiting hopefully for yet more liquidised baby food to be splattered over her gorgeous big face.

I honestly cannot remember exactly how many commands Cindy recognised in those days but, purely for illustrative purposes, the following is a selection of human words and phrases, each and every one of which both of my own two dogs, Tanna and Saffy, clearly understand today. For the record, I reckon that this selection represents less than one third of their full repertoire, so I hope it will give you an idea of their range of word perception. The meanings of most of these are self-evident, and I have only included an explanation where the verbal utterance is so completely bizarre that it would be impossible (and perhaps even psychologically harmful) for the reader to attempt to work it out for himself/herself.

Here goes.

Sit
Paw
Lie down
Come here
Stay
Side (walking by my side, in preference to the more established 'heel' command)
Fetch
Do you want to go a walk?
Who did that? (this is a real scolding statement, after a naughty misdeed)
No
Good dog / clever dog

Bad dog
Do you want your dinner?
Don't be cheeky (this is a mild scolding statement, after a bit of harmless mischief)
Do you want out?
Are we going for a pint? (or a packet of crisps, in the dogs' case)
Behave
Go and see (an invitation for them to run and check out who has just rung the doorbell)
Where's your toy? (an invitation to play)
Up-up (invites the dogs to put their front paws on our knees, so that they can get petted)
Where's the towel? (invites them to fetch their own, in order for me to dry them after they have been swimming, which is more or less always)
Go to bed
What's in the fridge? (invites them to come with me while I open the fridge door, where I have a treat waiting to be administered)
Get in the house
Where are we? (invites them to awake from their slumbers in the car, when we're approaching one of their favourite haunts)
Dead (the command for letting go of an object)
Where's your sore paw? (reassurance that I have clocked the cut or injured paw, if rather pathetic to behold)
Go and get a drink (important command for them to drink out of a stream or river, when I know that this will be the last drinking opportunity for a good few miles)
Go and do your business (command for them to do the toilet, on the rare occasion when they have not already done so)
Here comes trouble (invitation for them to run in and introduce themselves to whoever happens to be in the house, when they arrive back from a walk)
Go and get your leads

What do good dogs get? (reward time, on account of them doing a very clever thing)
Who's that? (alternative invitation for them to run to the door barking, when someone rings the bell or knocks the door)
Who's out there? (similar invitation, if the security light comes on at night)
Are we going in the car?
Work now (command for them to come and lie down quietly outside my office door, while I work at my desk)

So there you have it. My two big dogs can easily recognise and clearly understand well over one hundred words and commands today, as indeed could Cindy all those years ago. Alas, none of them could articulate a single one.

In my steadily progressing search for the linguistic holy grail of *Dogmanese* all that time ago, I knew with complete certainty that the answer would have much less to do with Cindy's mouth and ears.

And much more to do with the magic in her eyes.

On The Face Of It

'If a dog will not come to you after having looked you in the eye,
you should go home and examine your conscience.'
(Woodrow Wilson, 28th President of the United States)

Call me old smarty pants, but without even using any of those verbal commands, words or phrases that I listed in the previous chapter, I can easily convey certain messages to my two dogs today, simply by making a specific facial gesture. Here are a couple of examples.

If I'm sitting at my desk and typing away furiously on the keyboard, or just relaxing on the settee reading a newspaper, and all of a sudden I look up and stare at both dogs, opening my mouth ever-so-slightly, Tanna's eyes will light up in intrigue and expectation, while Saffy will tilt her head to one side, normally the left. If I hold that same gaze for any more than ten seconds, Tanna will get up, stretch her frame, start wagging her tail with increasing frequency and eventually bark at me, while Saffy will commence her silly routine of spinning around in circles. Both of them just instinctively know that the facial gesture they've just seen on their eccentric master's ageing *visage* is telling them that he's about to 'do something interesting', like take them out for a walk or play with their ball, for instance.

Alternatively, if I lower my eyebrows and screw up my wrinkled big face in a cross expression, which I am told is an increasingly common occurrence these days, both of them know for sure that they have done something that displeases me, such as tearing the fluff out of the new toys that Nan has just bought them for a tenner apiece, or scoffing the still-warm granary loaf that was lying innocently on the kitchen worktop awaiting conversion to my sandwiches.

The process works very well the other way around too, because I really can read my dogs' facial expressions like the proverbial book. If both of them have been lying at my feet for half an hour, with their chins flat on the floor and their big soulful eyes staring directly at me without even blinking for a microsecond, a visually-impaired Martian who had never even seen a dog before would be able to tell that they are bored senseless and wish me to inject some action into the proceedings. When Saffy saunters up to me, stretches herself, then stares at me with her mouth slightly open and panting gently, I know that she needs out for the toilet, while Tanna's customised procedure for asking out is a very similar facial expression, followed by her well-rehearsed routine of trotting back and forward around the general direction of the door.

I'm spending a wee bit of time rehearsing this particular matter simply because, having established that the non-verbal dimension of human-canine communication is of paramount importance, the dog's facial expression can be especially revealing, at least in my own experience anyway.

Cindy had one totally unique facial expression, which is very difficult to describe succinctly, but which was completely unmistakable and gloriously unforgettable. We called it her 'chase look'.

She normally adorned herself with her chase look when she had been charging around after a big stick in a field, or leaping and swimming over the cascading waves of Ayr beach, or in any situation where she was simply having great fun. It was almost as if once her adrenalin levels hit a certain 'tipping point', her face just took over.

Somehow, the chase look contrived to present itself simultaneously as eye-poppingly hilarious and unsettlingly scary, simply because we knew for sure that Cindy was about to do something quite outrageous, and yet we were completely oblivious as to precisely which form that behaviour might take.

We would only ever see Cindy's chase look when a number of physical conditions prevailed, that number being precisely three. First of all, she had to be off the leash; secondly, she had to have manoeuvred herself onto the 'wrong' side of me; and finally, there had to be an audience for her to play up to, the more the merrier in fact.

It was an expression that said, quite simply, 'There is absolutely no bloody way that you're putting that leash on me. And as far as jumping back into the car goes, you can forget it. And, by the way, how about trying to catch me, because I fancy a bit of a chase around the park right now, which I will inevitably win, and which will make you look like a complete plonker in front of all these people. So come on, big man.'

Her rationale was simplicity itself. Once she had managed to create the ideal set of circumstances in which to make me look like a bloody fool for the delectation of everyone who happened to be in the vicinity, she would then catch my eye and press green for go. In fact, so clinical were her motives, and so superbly thought-out her preparations, that she invariably gave one almighty 'WOOF!' simply to attract anyone who hadn't already been watching her antics, thereby maximising her potential audience before the curtain went up on her command performance. What a mischievous little bastard she could be, but the thing was that everybody simply adored her.

One Sunday afternoon, after just such an episode of wanton mayhem in Ayr's wonderful Belleisle Park, a Welsh guy called Evan came up to me, tears of laughter still streaming down his face, and shook my hand then actually suggested that Cindy and I should advertise to perform at children's birthday parties and the like. He said that he hadn't laughed so much for years, and that we could make a bloody fortune if we really put our minds to it. Had he not been built like the archetypal muscle-bound Taffy rugby player, I might well have decked him there and then for his unintentional insolence. I still laugh out loud when I recall that unmistakeable magic twinkle in Cindy's eyes, an expression that radiated pure mischief, but absolutely no malice.

Cindy was actually a very well-behaved young dog most of the time, but never when her beautiful big golden face suddenly metamorphosed to take on the dreaded chase look. The problem for Nan and me was that it just took us such a ridiculously long time before the penny eventually dropped that Cindy had to have manufactured the aforementioned 'three conditions' before the riotous nonsense would commence. And it was so simple, really. As easy as one-two-three in fact.

She had to be free, she had to have a clear exit route, and she had to have an audience. So much so, that if only two of the three conditions were met, Cindy wouldn't even bother trying. For example, if her leash was over her neck, no problem. If her exit route was blocked and she had nowhere to go, ditto. If there was no one around for her to show off to, there was no point in her even bothering to go to the effort. What a calculating little madam she was, when I think about it.

The tales of Cindy's chase look were legend, they really were. She once had me running the length and breadth of Tralee Bay, just north of the beautiful west coast seaside town of Oban, while she cavorted around like a bloody idiot for what seemed like ages, and leapt up on a succession of dog-phobic picknickers, nicking their tuna sandwiches *en passant*, as I lumbered after her in hopeless pursuit.

One summer's evening, while we had been entertaining a few friends at a barbecue in our own back garden, the chase look suddenly materialised quite out of the blue and, trust me, I have chosen the word 'entertained' very carefully. It must have taken me a full hour to get Cindy back into the house. That particular evening, she simply ran amok, and by the time I eventually got hold of her, my vegetable garden looked as if it had been hit by a freak tornado and our guests were literally crying their eyes out in helpless laughter. Nan told me a few days later that one of her friends, a physiotherapist called Jane, had actually wet herself, then deliberately spilled her gin-and-tonic on my patio to conceal the evidence and spare her own embarrassment.

On another occasion, when Nan had been feeling rather poorly and the family GP had called in to see her, Cindy again manufactured the pre-requisite 'three conditions', before assuming her chase look. Being in her own home, she was of course unrestrained (thereby satisfying <u>Condition 1</u>), she managed to position herself between the back door (which had been inadvertently left open by the doctor) and myself, thus providing a handy exit route (<u>Condition 2</u>), and she had identified a small-but-captive audience (<u>Condition 3</u>). When I saw her chase look developing, I just roared, 'CINDY, NO!' about one microsecond before the little beggar grabbed his car keys off the kitchen table and bolted down the steps, back up which she would be dragged by the scruff of the neck about thirty minutes later, by which time at least three of the poor chap's other patients would no doubt have passed away prematurely.

One rainy afternoon, it was Nan herself who was to be the exasperated recipient of Cindy's chase look. There we were in the car, Nan dropping me off at the town square with my obligatory shopping list and other associated 'things to do'. As I nipped out of the front passenger's door, Nan sat in the driver's seat with Cindy lying in the back. It was only when Nan decided to wind down the rear window that she noticed Cindy sitting up, then the chase look bursting out of her eyes like sunflowers in full bloom. At first Nan was a bit confused, but then the spectacular reality dawned on her. 'CINDY, NO!' she screamed, just in time to see our beloved pet's backside spring out of the back window. A few minutes later, Cindy introduced herself to me at the cheese counter in the local supermarket.

If the chase look was the most spectacular of all, then there were umpteen other facial expressions which readily gave the game away as to how Cindy was feeling, even to the point of somehow managing at times to let me know what she was actually thinking.

The thing about dogs' expressions is that they are almost always involuntary, and it is these that really tell the true story. While humans can manufacture voluntary facial expressions to conceal their true feelings or even to deceive others, dogs simply cannot, at least in my experience anyway. Therefore, when

Cindy made a facial gesture, it honestly was like witnessing her innermost thoughts being illuminated by a searchlight.

It is, of course, the case that a dog's facial expressions cannot really be read accurately or interpreted reliably without also factoring into the equation its body posture, and the position and behaviour of its limbs, ears, tail and so on. However, for me at least, it was always Cindy's face, and particularly her eyes, that told the real story and managed to let me know whether she was happy or sad, excited or worried, healthy or under the weather.

Now I fully appreciate that any of our professional veterinary experts, animal psychologists and canine behavioural buffs who are wading their way through this stuff might be sitting there, shaking their heads and tut-tutting their disapproving way from page to page, in their superior opinion that I am over-simplifying matters somewhat. That is as may be, but then they should always remember that this book was never intended to be an academic thesis.

It is, though, an attempt to explain in some quasi-scientific but completely honest way, and as far as is rationally possible, just how I actually managed to learn to communicate at a pretty advanced level with a ten-quid puppy, and how our remarkable 'connection' really changed my life at a time when I badly needed a trusted and objective philosopher.

Cindy may have developed the knack of speaking with her mouth shut, but to me her face was always a window into her soul.

The Spectre In The Snowstorm

'Dreams are true while they last, and do we not live in dreams?'
(Alfred Lord Tennyson)

On the very last day of each calendar year, or 'Hogmanay' as we canny Scots more aptly refer to it, Cindy and I would always head for the hills on a marathon trek.

There was never any overtly specific rationale for this annual ritual, although it probably had something to do with me trying to self-justify my planned over-indulgence in the early hours of the following morning whilst bringing in the New Year, by convincing myself that I would have burned up so many calories whilst plodding over the moors that my subsequent alcohol intake would simply be cancelled out by my earlier exertions. Please do not attempt to work out my thinking here, because it will only cause you untold confusion and, anyway, I could hardly follow it myself at the time.

Hogmanay had always been a very special day for family, friends and indeed the wider Cumnock community for as long as I could remember, and that particular day of the year still retains a rather unique place in the Scottish social and cultural calendar, even if it is now somewhat diminished in feverishness and eccentricity.

I have countless and quite wonderful memories of the preparations that heralded each successive New Year, always an auspicious occasion that brought with it the customary mix of happy and sad reflections of the year just gone, and hopes and fears for the one ahead.

I vividly remember, as a mere six-year-old, being plied with my Granny's very own home-made ginger wine and shortbread, while my parents and our 'first footers' – near neighbours and friends who would drop in, uninvited but eagerly expected, to 'bring in the new' – refilled each others' glasses for the umpteenth time with a few more drops of the *Bold John Barleycorn*.

Meanwhile, the entertainment would be provided by crackly recordings of the *Jimmy Shand* band belting out their highly invigorating Scottish country dance music, which unfailingly got everyone up on their feet and cavorting around to such indigenous dance classics as *The Gay Gordons* and *Strip The Willow*, but interspersed with the inevitable would-be opera singers who, as soon as they got to their unsteady feet, immediately killed the party mood once more in order to play out their own self-indulgent quasi-musical fantasies. Indeed, on one particular occasion, I remember everyone whoopin'-an'-hollerin' to some riotous fiddle tune one minute, and then sitting down sobbing their eyes out to our next door neighbour Charlie's wrist-slitting version of *'Nobody's Child'* the very next. Hogmanay was a very bewildering time for a young lad.

Then as the years went on, and as my own maturing taste buds gradually nudged me on a fascinating journey from ginger wine-and-shortbread to whisky-and-soda-and-mutton pies, I eventually came out the other side as the wide-eyed party-goer, replacing the former whingeing-faced party-pooper. And I must say that, from the age of about sixteen onwards, Hogmanay really became a bit of a hoot for me, largely I think because I happened to have acquired a pretty enormous circle of mates who were almost as crazy as I was, but wonderful friends into the bargain.

I suppose I did actually mature a little bit when I eventually succumbed to Nan's marital clutches, but given that she herself had been a bit of a nutter until her illness struck, her remedial influence on my social shenanigans was somewhat limited from the outset. Around that time, we all took turns to host the annual Hogmanay bash, with each particular year's hostess making all the grub, and the multitudinous first-footers arriving no earlier than twelve-thirty but no later than one-thirty, and equipped with a big shopping bag containing a selection of spirits, some of their own grannies' black bun and fruit cake, and a lump of coal for good luck. Normally, the New Year party ended around eight o'clock in the morning, although I do once remember Nan and I staggering our way home just in time for lunch at my parents' house the following day. Hogmanay and New Year's Day really were great fun in those days, but probably not all that kind to our various anatomical organs.

And so it was against this highly-cultured backdrop, that Cindy and I got ourselves all happed up and ready to face the icy north-easterly winds, as we set off towards our annual hike through the Ayrshire wilderness. Before we did so, I was delighted to be reminded by Nan that it was my best mate Euan's turn to host the Hogmanay shindig that particular year. Therefore, all I would have to do when Cindy and I returned some four hours later, was to have a bath, put my feet up for an hour or two, eat the hearty dinner that Nan would have made for me, and then get the carry-out ready for transportation to nearby Craigens. Happy days.

Little did Cindy and I know at the time that this would really be a Hogmanay to remember, but not for the reasons we had expected.

So I filled the vacuum flask with hot tea, and slipped it into my rucksack along with the roast chicken sandwiches that Nan had prepared and put into tinfoil for us, then chucked in a big bottle of water together with a collapsible plastic dish for Cindy to drink out of, and a handful of biscuits for her to gorge upon, hopefully to distract her while I was trying to eat the sandwiches. Some bloody hope.

It was later than I had intended by the time we eventually managed to set off, about eleven o'clock in fact, mainly due to the fact that my nearest-and-dearest had despatched me to the local supermarket to perform the New Year shopping chores, which by that stage Nan was simply no longer physically able to do by herself, God love her.

With Cindy half-sitting and half-standing on the back seat in eagle-eyed expectation, I drove through my childhood village of Logan, and on towards the Glenmuir valley. As I passed Dalblair Bridge, a nostalgic shudder ran up my spine, and I cast a quick glance in the rear view mirror, only to see Cindy's big eyes looking back at me.

'Stop fidgeting, I told you everything would be fine,' they seemed to say.

By the time we had reached the end of the tarmac road, and parked the car on the grass verge opposite the gamekeeper's cottage, a few pretty large flakes of snow had already begun to fall, and the sky was beginning to take on that very distinctive dark orange-grey hue that can only signal yet more of the white stuff.

I thought nothing of it at the time, and neither did Cindy as she bolted out of the back door with an ear-splitting 'WOOF! WOOF!' which was immediately drowned out by reciprocal and synchronised barking from the dozen or so magnificent-looking big black Labrador gun dogs that the 'keeper housed in a huge enclosure adjacent to his own cottage.

Less than ten minutes later, we had begun to follow the Shaw Burn, one of the hillside tributaries that flows into the River Lugar, which itself then feeds the mighty River Ayr. When we reached the second sharp corner in the burn, I knew from past experience that we could cut up the gentle hillside and onto the higher terrain, where Cindy could then roam freely beside me for as long as she pleased.

The plan was that we would walk for a maximum of one-and-a-half-hours in the general direction of the village of New Cumnock, some three miles away as the crow flies, in order that we could make our return journey well before dark, which would be around four o'clock at that time of year. Although there were various well-trodden footpaths along the way, there was never any adventure in following someone else's boot prints, so we headed further up the slope to virgin pastures, since I was confident that I knew the landscape reasonably well. The only thing that niggled at me a wee bit was the fact that the snow, by now, was beginning to get considerably heavier, and starting to settle on the ground.

'No problem, Cindy!' I shouted, as I made yet another enormous snowball with my bare and by-now numbing hands, and threw it up into the air. 'Scott didn't need a bloody footpath to find his way to the South Pole!'

Cindy again sprang gleefully into the air, and grabbed the snowball in her mouth as it made its descent, where it suffered the same disintegrating fate as its half dozen or so watery predecessors. She was having a ball, and so was her infantile master.

About an hour or so later, we reached some old brick kilns that I recognised from my teenage days, since these were located just a few hundred metres away from a very secluded spot on the single-track B-road from New Cumnock to Kirkconnel, where my equally single-track mind had once succeeded in luring a few former girlfriends to spend an hour or two snogging and fumbling under various hippy-style garments.

I looked at my watch. It was now quarter-past-one, which I quickly calculated would allow us about half an hour for lunch and a further trek of about three times that duration, which would in turn get us back to the car well before dark. So off came the rucksack, and out came the tea and chicken lunch, not forgetting the dog biscuits in which it soon became clear that Cindy had no interest whatsoever. She wanted my sandwiches, end of story.

It had begun to get very cold indeed that afternoon, and I was really pleased to have wrapped myself up accordingly. I remember, in particular, the boiling hot tea from the vacuum flask immediately turning lukewarm as soon as it hit the plastic cup.

'I think we're going to have a bloody cold January, Cindy,' I remarked, as she gobbled on the last remaining crust of what was supposed to be my lunch, not hers. I stuffed the uneaten dog biscuits into my waterproof jacket pocket for future inducement of canine obedience.

'Right, let's head back to Dalblair!' I announced, after having taken a leak, and then washing my hands in the snow that was now both billowing around our heads and beginning to drift along the near-frozen ground, by virtue of the rapidly increasing icy winds.

Cindy gave another resounding 'WOOF! WOOF!' and darted out in front of me as I began trying to re-trace my footprints, in lieu of the more familiar but by now almost obliterated landscape. I could just make out the shapes that my walking boots had made in the snow only an hour or so previously and also, to my huge amusement, the much smaller ones that Cindy's paws had formed themselves, and which veered off at umpteen enormous tangents right and left, to provide me with irrefutable evidence that her own walks normally stretched to at least double the distance of my own. We managed to retrace what was left of our footprints for no more than about forty minutes, by which time they had all but disappeared in the thickening snowdrifts.

It was only then that the potential peril of our situation dawned on me for the very first time. We could get bloody lost out here, I mumbled to myself in complete silence, to avoid causing any anxiety to Cindy.

She immediately stopped and stared at me.

'What do you mean we could get lost?' her eyes enquired, as yet more snowflakes settled on her jet-black nose, before melting from her body heat. Somehow, I wasn't in the slightest bit surprised that she had read my thoughts verbatim. After all, she always could do.

I tried my best to look out for familiar landmarks, such as distinctive hilltops, the occasional oddly-shaped tree, an old section of derelict wooden fencing and so on, but the situation was deteriorating rapidly as the snowfall developed into a blizzard, and the sky became darker and darker. About twenty-five minutes later, we had walked almost the same distance back, and I realised that if we were really heading in the right direction, I should be starting to recognise some of the more obvious features around the general area of the Shaw Burn.

I stopped and did a panoramic three-hundred-and-sixty-degree sweep, sheltering my eyes from the snow flakes with the palms of both hands. Nothing, absolutely nothing did I recognise. All around was snow, snow and more bloody snow.

And it was at that point, that the scary reality of the situation hit me. Here we both were, stuck in the middle of nowhere in a freezing blizzard, with no shelter, no compass, no means of communication, about one hour of gloomy daylight remaining, and approximately eight dog biscuits between us to supply the energy that would need to see us through the night. Mind you, we did seem to be well enough provided for on the drinking water front, as innumerable cubic miles of snow could readily testify.

Cindy began to sense my alarm which, by that stage, was not all that short of embryonic panic. In a valiant but singularly unsuccessful attempt to lighten the mood, I looked at her and laughed, 'Don't worry, lass, we've got to get home to eat all that bloody shortbread tonight!'

Cindy wasn't for laughing, though. She knew the score.

I decided to park my already-saturated backside down on the stump of a long-deceased tree, and Cindy sat down beside me. She was panting heavily, which clearly signalled to me that she was becoming quite agitated by the various subliminal signals she was picking up from me. This was definitely not a good situation.

'What do you think, Cindy?' I asked her, more in desperation than expectation this time, despite my supreme confidence in her customary powers of cognitive perception. Cindy just looked back at me, expressionless. So thick was the snow by then, that I couldn't even see her eyes, let alone attempt to decipher what, if anything, her pupils were trying to tell me.

Recognising the critical time imperative that loomed large in our dire situation, I immediately stood back up and repeated the question. 'What do you think, Cindy?'

And just at that, her body posture began to change. Her

entire skeletal frame appeared to turn rigid, and her tail began to point straight backwards with its very tip quivering. By this time, her panting had completely stopped and her mouth was closed, although her top lip began to curl ever-so-slightly. I watched in amazement as her hackles began to rise, first on the small of her back, then radiating upwards to her nape and head, and finally downwards all the way along her tail.

'Cindy, what is it, lass?' I asked. 'You're starting to spook me.'

'WOW! WOW! WOW! WOW! WOW!'

I froze to the spot.

Cindy began staring over my shoulder, into the distance.

'Cindy, what the bloody hell is it?' I asked nervously, before spinning around. And there, on the distant horizon, I could just make out a shape.

It was the shape of a man. He appeared to be very elderly, with a decidedly stooped posture, and he was leaning on some kind of walking stick. Somehow he seemed strangely familiar, but by that time the conditions were so dreadful that I could no longer even trust my own eyes. I then entertained another thought that was considerably less appealing than the apparition on the horizon. Perhaps I was hallucinating.

As Cindy continued growling and barking, obviously every bit as spooked as I was by that stage, the strange figure suddenly began waving and pointing his arms to his left, which since we were now both facing him, was to our right.

I shouted towards him, 'WE'RE LOST! WE'RE TRYING TO GET BACK TO DALBLAIR!'

Whether he heard me or not through the whistling wind, I will never know, but he just continued waving his arms and pointing in the same direction. Still Cindy continued to bark, her hackles by this time almost vertical. I turned in the direction the old man was pointing, and then took a few steps up the slight incline, signalling Cindy to follow me.

After about thirty metres or so, I had reached the brow of the little hill, and there straight in front of me was the magnificent sight of the Shaw Burn. Slightly further away in the gloomy distance, I could just make out the contours of the gamekeeper's cottage at Dalblair Bridge. I honestly could have cried with relief.

I pulled up my sleeve, wiped some flakes of snow off my watch, and saw that it was just after three o'clock. By my reckoning, we still had about a mile-and-a-half to go, but at least another half hour of remaining daylight in which to negotiate our way through the eerie blizzard. In sincere gratitude, I turned around again to wave my thanks to our sinister old saviour.

He was nowhere to be seen.

Despite the fact that he had been walking over a pancake-flat area of the moor at the time, he was gone. It was as if he had never even been there in the first place.

'WOW! WOW! WOW! WOW! WOW!' Cindy howled again in his direction, her hackles still standing to attention.

'Shut up Cindy, for Christ's sake!' I rebuked her. 'That old geezer might just have saved our lives.' I was never one for gratuitous blasphemy, but on that day, believe me, the separation between the earthly and the spiritual was almost indistinguishable.

About nine hours later, and almost five hundred miles southwards in the nation's capital, Big Ben's mighty bells chimed in the New Year. As Nan, Cindy and I hugged and kissed each other in our living room, we all prayed silently that, please God, it would be a good one. Another hour later, I was jigging around to a *Speyside Reel*, with Euan's wife Margaret in one hand and a glass of *The Famous Grouse* whisky in the other.

By ten o'clock the next morning and having managed only four hours' proper sleep in bed, I found myself lying in my big armchair trying to doze off a dreadful hangover. And that was when I awoke from one of the most vivid and blisteringly realistic dreams I had ever experienced.

'IT WAS MY PAPA!' I shouted, as I shot bolt upright in my seat.

'Oh my God!' gasped Nan, spilling her coffee. 'Ian, what are you talking about? I nearly jumped out of my skin there. Have you been dreaming?'

'CINDY, IT WAS MY PAPA WHO SAVED US!' I shouted again, this time looking straight at my canine soulmate, my heart thumping like a drum. Cindy's hackles began bristling along her spine. I could hardly catch my breath.

We both looked at each other, and then immediately realised that there was no need for any further discussion on the matter.

Dogmanese was always a language that was best spoken in silence.

The Eyes Have It

'My sunshine doesn't come from the skies, it comes from the love in my dog's eyes.'
(Anon)

I suppose dogs' faces always fascinated me, to be fair. They just always seem to radiate such genuine openness and complete honesty, whether signalling love, loyalty, fear or even loathing. Openness and honesty that, in our own human race, is seldom displayed other than on the faces of very young children.

Ever since that fateful day in my early childhood, when I witnessed at first hand the very life being kicked out of a poor, innocent little mongrel simply because her master had been having a bad day in the kitchen, I had been totally captivated by our best friend, the dog. And till the day I die, I will never be able to extinguish the image of that poor little dog's anguished face from my mind.

Mind you, it's a very strange thing the face, isn't it? Well at least I think so anyway. When you look at the faces of most animals on this little planet of ours, you must admit that they tend to follow the same old winning formula, the prototype of which was presumably designed around the dawn of time, with the process of evolution then refining them over many billions of years.

When you think about it, most earthly creatures, and certainly almost all mammals, tend to have four distinct but craftily inter-related features located on or around the face, these being the ears, the eyes, the nose and the mouth. And presumably for very good reason too, which I understand is to oversee the administration of body fuel to give us the energy we need to survive, or food as we tend to call it these days.

Have you ever studied a baby's face at feeding time? I have, you know, because at the time of writing this book, my delightful first granddaughter, Anna, was around seven months old, and had just been introduced to 'solids'. So one day, I decided to study the dynamics involved. What a clinical old grandfather I can be at times, don't you think? And let me assure you, I've been called a lot worse. Very crudely, the baby-feeding dynamics appeared to me as to present as follows.

As little Anna sits propped up in her multi-coloured high-chair, the word 'dinner' is mentioned along with a few other key expressions that she is beginning to recognise. The ears spring into action, causing the whole face to look extremely interested. The eyes light up at the very sight of a gooey mush of pureed carrots and sweet potato, or some other such similar concoction that you and I would never even dream of putting anywhere near our mouths. The nose twitches and signals excited approval to the face, which then starts beaming in anticipation. The mouth opens willingly, as the little plastic spoon approaches, and the stuff is shovelled in by her mother (only to make its slimy reappearance a few seconds later, as it dribbles down her chin).

Utterly revolting really, but scientifically fascinating nevertheless. And all because we have just witnessed a helpless young baby demonstrating why the face is actually designed the way it is, which is to oversee the whole process of ingestion of food that is safe enough to eat. In effect, the face controls four of the five senses (sight, sound, taste and smell), while the fifth (touch) is necessarily a bit more multi-faceted than that. The good lord put a bit of thought into the whole process, you know.

Of course, while the above four organs are located on each animal's face, their actual and relative locations can vary quite a bit from species to species, and none more strikingly so than the eyes. Fortunately, you and I tend to veer towards the safe end of mother nature's great food chain, and so we have front-facing eyes, just like lions, tigers and other animals that prey upon those who are a bit less fortunate, as the latter strut their last stuff along the plains, only to end up in the digestive tracts of the former. On the other hand, those a bit further down the food chain, such as rabbits and mice - who might be described more accurately as the dinner rather than the diner - tend to have side-facing eyes in order to provide them with near-panoramic vision, with which to afford them an early warning detection system (which plainly doesn't always work, now does it?).

Mercifully, dogs are pretty close to the top end of the chain, since whether or not your pet pooch is a Red Setter, a Golden Retriever or a Toy Poodle, he or she is still descended from Mister Wolf himself, and it's better just to keep that little bit of information up your sleeve for future reference (if you get my drift). We may over many centuries have mucked about with our dogs' physical characteristics, messed around with their minds, taught them to carry out specialist jobs of work and trained them to perform silly tricks, but at the end of the day all dogs are still very much 'wolves in sheep's clothing', and we should never, ever forget that quaint little scientific fact.

So now we all know exactly where we stand in the food chain, don't we? And if we've all been paying attention, we also know why God gave us faces, which was actually to help us to survive, rather than to adorn our assorted big coupons with designer stubble, metallic studs and makeup. Is my technical jargon getting too demanding for you?

It's not? Excellent, then I'll press on.

The mouth, eyes, ears and nose all play a very important part in the communication process as well, of course, with the last two also having performed a vital role in my own life since I was six years old, which was to hold my spectacles in place, without which I would almost certainly not have reached seven. Indeed, I've often wondered if my own appallingly poor eyesight had anything to do with my fascination with Cindy's eyes. So with that little snippet of confused self-reflection, let's now have an even closer look at the eye itself, shall we?

The eye – and I'm afraid I'm going to get even more technical here – is composed of many different parts. I refer to them as *'bits'*. Do try to stay with me.

The hole in the middle that lets the light in is called the *pupil*, the coloured part around the pupil is called the *iris*, and it is actually the iris that expands and contracts with impressive frequency to control the amount of light that gets in. (So there you go, and you thought it was actually the pupil that did this, didn't you?) Finally, the whites of our eyes are called the *sclera*, and the eyelids are referred to in medical jargon as *eyelids*, which continually open and close all through our waking hours to wash tears over the eyeballs and keep them clean. Still with me?

The important thing about our pupils is this, though. Not only do they expand and contract in response to varying degrees of darkness and sunlight, but they also react to a range of other stimuli as well. It is this that really does allow the eyes to 'speak volumes'. And it was this which I am absolutely certain was the key to Cindy sending me signals and messages that I gradually learned to recognise and understand.

The fact of the matter is that our pupils can also dilate directly as a result of certain other external stimuli, such as keen interest in the proceedings, deep emotions and high excitement, whereas the opposite process of contraction is a response to such things as relaxation, tiredness or even boredom. Apparently, we tend to be attracted to a significant other when his or her pupils are dilated, since this radiates genuine interest and feeling, while we become switched off by another whose pupils have contracted, because that signals someone who is both disinterested and uninteresting.

I'm sure you will be able to recall certain situations in which another person has been radiating keen interest in you, perhaps even of a romantic nature, purely through eye contact. In such a scenario, you will probably have failed to notice the constant dilation-contraction patterns of their pupils, since you will no doubt have been concentrating on checking out one or two other interesting shapes and dimensions. However, it will almost certainly have been their dilated pupils which have been sending you a subliminal, but very strong signal that your luck might be in, if you just play your cards right. Indeed, the very reason that a candlelit dinner for two can be tremendously aphrodisiacal, is that the low light causes both sets of pupils to dilate, signalling interest and physical attractiveness to each other.

So for the guys out there, now you know. Dim the lights, light the candles, put your specs on and get the condoms out of the sock drawer.

Many a canine research paper has quite clearly demonstrated that you can tell a great deal about a dog's well-being, and even its innermost feelings, by looking at its face and, in particular, its eyes. On a personal level, I had already come to that conclusion anyway, as a direct consequence of my recent surreal connection in the car with Cindy, and so all that my associated desktop reading really achieved was to provide me with an evidence-based rationale for my optimistic self-fulfilling prophecy. I just knew that it was Cindy's eyes that were telling me these things. It was the intensity of her gaze, the absence of blinking over an inordinately lengthy period, and the frequency and dynamics of her pupil dilation-contraction reflexes that were sending me these strange messages. Absolutely no doubt about it.

The problem was, though, that Cindy actually had particularly dark eyes, and fairly small sclera, which meant that I could barely make out her pupil dilation pattern when she was gazing directly at me, although I could do so much more clearly when she was positioned at a very slight angle, which had certainly been the case on that red-letter day in the car. I found that even the tiniest angle made all the difference in helping me to detect her darker pupil movement against the much lighter contrast of the 'whites' of her eyes. And so from that point onwards, I always tried to position myself ever-so-slightly to the side of Cindy, rather than head-on, when we were having one of our 'conversations'.

Anyway it seemed to work, because I soon learned to read her eyes more and more accurately and intuitively. In fact, quite often, and rather scarily too I suppose, I often found that I could tell what Cindy was about to do before she actually did it, and purely from the look in her eyes. Such episodes were always characterised by a very brief sensation that time itself had been put on hold, and there always seemed to be a split second between me clocking which particular mischievous course of action she had decided to pursue this time around, and the execution of the riotous misdeed itself.

By way of illustration, please permit me to tell you about two quite separate incidents that occurred within an hour of each other, a couple of days before Christmas in the late 'seventies, at a time when Nan had been going through a particularly bad time with her illness. I remember that she was very, very low indeed that day, and really struggling to come to terms with the depressingly progressive nature of her disability. So she decided to do what she still does to this very day when something is troubling her. She set about doing some housework.

Having already washed the clothes, vacuumed the carpets and polished the furniture, she then decided to begin preparing a pot of home-made soup, based on a recipe handed down by her late grandmother. It was my very own favourite 'kidney broth', and the procedure involved preparing and mixing all the vegetables together with a whole ox kidney, before simmering the mixture together in a large soup pot on our kitchen stove. Once the soup was more or less ready, which would be at least two hours later, she would then remove the kidney from the pot to let it cool down a bit, so that she could grate the meat into small bite-sized pieces and return these to the pot. I can still remember the glorious smell to this day of what was a quintessentially Scottish, but absolutely delicious soup.

So there we all were, Nan sitting and me standing in our kitchen, waiting for her to finish the procedure so that we could get stuck into the grub, when all of a sudden I noticed that completely unmistakable look in Cindy's eyes. It was one of pure unadulterated mischief, and time just stood still, if only for a nanosecond. By the time I had managed to snap back into life again, the whole kidney was already making its intact way down Cindy's gullet *en route* to her stomach. As she smacked her lips, I smacked her arse, and Nan and I then fell about laughing. Our darling big dog really was the best psychological therapy Nan could ever have wished for, even if her actions did occasionally detract from the nutritional quality of our dinner table.

Less than an hour later that same day, one of the local GPs despatched himself to our house on a routine visit. He rang the doorbell just as Nan and I were about to sit down to a big bowl of her newly-made, kidney-free, kidney broth. It would have to wait. I opened the door with Cindy leaping around by my side as usual, ushered the doctor into the living room and waited for Nan to wheel herself through. As the guy carried out a superficial examination and chatted to Nan about how she was keeping, Cindy just sat protectively by her side, as she always sensed the need to do whenever she was down-in-the-mouth, which was a pretty regular condition in those days.

Then, just as the poor man began to pack his things back into his little black case, I saw it again, that completely unmistakeable twinkle in Cindy's eyes, and thought, 'Oh no! Oh shit!' Once again, time just appeared to freeze, and she absolutely bolted towards him. As I stood there in some kind of transient catatonic state, she sprang up into the air, grabbed the stethoscope that was dangling over his shoulders and bolted up the stairs, no doubt to hide the bloody thing under the bed beside her latest cache of stolen goods. She really was the giddy limit.

Cindy's eyes had been 'telling me things' for some time by that stage, and at least I now knew that there was a rational scientific explanation for much of what had happened ever since the prophetic incident in the car at Dalblair Bridge. However, I was also fairly certain that there was something else going on here, which simply had to be some kind of 'sixth sense' activity at play, and which was still awaiting persuasive elucidation. All that mattered, for the time being at least, was that I had acquired a much better understanding of the main factors that influenced the flow of information between *Homo Sapien* and *Canis Familiaris*, and a wee bit of reassurance that I might not have lost my marbles after all.

I resolved to keep my eyes open. As they say.

Harnessing Cindy Power

'After climbing a great hill, one only finds that there are many more hills to climb,'
(Nelson Mandela)

So there it was then, another quaint little personal dilemma.

On the one hand, I had acquired the canine companion of my dreams, the dog I had craved since I was ten years old. Cindy was a gorgeous big Labrador bitch with a glorious golden coat, a magnificent forehead, a beautiful happy face, silky ears and an equally silky tail which seemed to wag furiously from dawn till dusk, spilling every cup of tea and destroying every precious ornament with which it came into contact. However, it was her eyes that defined her personality, eyes that seemed to radiate intelligence, happiness, fun, compassion and canine-human empathy in equal measure, any single component of which could be turned on and off as with the garden hosepipe, and like my hopelessly pathetic vegetable garden, just as the occasion demanded. Okay, she had been a real challenge as a puppy, particularly when it had come to the little matter of obedience training, which she had succeeded in completely redefining, but she really was the apple of my eye. I was just so very proud of Cindy, and I loved her dearly.

Even now that she was nearly three years old, and 'a big dog now' as Nan and I used to attempt to convince all three of us, she was still consumed by adolescent nonsense, and her whole *raison d'etre* seemed to revolve around exhausting the entire spectrum of canine mischievousness.

However, and against all of my earlier expectations, I had recently witnessed at first hand Cindy's amazing ability to communicate with me on an emotional and psychological level, about which I was steadily beginning to learn a great deal more, but the full extent of which I still could not completely comprehend. All I knew for sure was that I was extremely grateful for this bizarre connection. Whatever the imaginary Meg had done for my desperately sagging spirits the night before my first day at secondary school all those years ago, the real and very much alive Cindy had eclipsed several times over.

On the other hand, I had recently learned that my twenty-five-year-old wife of just three years, with whom I was very much in love, had contracted an incurable disease, and would very probably be in a wheelchair within a few months. In fact, the early prognosis had already convinced me that Nan could well be hopelessly bedridden just in time to deliver the baby she was carrying so lovingly in her womb, but so unsteadily on her feet.

So, as I sat one morning on the back door step with my coffee in one hand and my daft big dog's gorgeous head in the other, I said aloud, 'Where does this leave us now then, Cindy?'

Cindy turned her head towards me, stared at me for a moment or two, then licked the tip of my nose, which in itself was no great accomplishment on account of the size of that particular appendage. My earlier research had told me that when a dog licks a human, it is not really 'kissing' the person as such, but merely trying to establish important information such as physical condition, emotional mood and so on. You could have fooled me.

I continued speaking to her and gently stroking her ears. Every now and again she would yawn, turn and look at me, look away again, yawn and start the whole process all over again. I repeated the question.

'Cindy.' She turned and looked straight at me.

'Cindy, where does this leave us?' I asked.

Her eyes still stared. 'Cindy?' I asked rhetorically.

Her head tilted, first to one side then to the other. She held my gaze for a few moments, then looked away again, yawned and began scratching her face with the big sharp claws adorning her hind leg. I heard the click of my next door neighbour's back door opening, and stared straight ahead, as big Stewart came out with a briefcase in one hand and his packed lunch in the other. The door key was wedged between his teeth.

I began to internalise the subliminal messages that Cindy had transmitted to me only a few moments ago, through God-knows-what particular communicative channel this time. There seemed to be three of them.

1. I know how you're feeling, and I'm feeling the same way too.
2. Everything will be all right, so stop fretting, or you'll have me fretting too.
3. Nan is in for a tough time, and it's not going to be nice, but we are where we are, so we have to deal with it, and be strong for her.

I scratched my head and laughed out loud. How do you do that, Cindy, I wondered? How the hell do you manage to tell me these things? And without even opening your mouth?

'And what can you possibly find funny at this time on a bloody Monday morning?' Stewart asked with a frown.

Cindy immediately bolted down the steps towards him, and jumped up with her front paws on the fence. 'Hiya, Cindy, the big man lost his marbles again, has he?' enquired Stewart, somewhat rhetorically.

As he leaned over to pat Cindy, she wagged her tail and sniffed at the plastic bag he was carrying. She's not trying to detect or process a web of profound information this time, I thought silently, she's trying to nick his gammon sandwiches.

'Oh, I was just having a wee conversation with my dog,' I replied, still giggling away to myself.

'Aye, well you'll probably get a lot more sense out of Cindy than you'll get from your Chemistry pupils this morning, if they're anything like my lot in Geography,' he opined grumpily, obviously not in his best form, as he trudged off to his teaching duties somewhat further afield than my own, at that stage in our respective careers.

'You'll never know how true that is,' I chuckled. Stewart just shook his head dolefully, as he slumped wearily into his seriously clapped-out car.

Cindy skipped back up the steps and sat down beside me again. I looked at her and stroked her head. 'It's all right for you,' I said. 'You can crawl back into your lazy bed now, and curl up beside the bloody radiator. Or sharpen some more table legs for us if you get bored. But I'm afraid that Nan and I need to get our backsides in gear and get to work. Somebody's got to earn enough dough to keep you on *Winalot*.'

She tilted her head in instant recognition of an eminently familiar word that had just come tumbling out of my mouth. *Winalot?* Now you're talkin', big man.

Just how the hell am I managing to pick up these strange messages, I pondered, although a bit more seriously this time? Am I simply thinking these thoughts for Cindy and transmitting them back to a very willing and receptive brain, which is so tired that it will gladly interpret any little morsel of information as a message of hope? Of course I am, I concluded.

So I continued the kidology. 'Cindy, I'll give you a biscuit right now, if you just tell me what you're thinking.'

She looked at me eagerly and started speaking to me again with her big bright eyes, as some doggy saliva began to drip from her mouth in anticipation of imminent administration of my part of the bargain.

'A biscuit? Right, you're on,' she said. 'I'm thinking that we're going to invent *Cindy Power*.'

'*Cindy Power?*' I asked with a puzzled frown. 'What the hell is *Cindy Power*, Cindy?'

'Oh, you'll find out soon. Now, where's that biscuit you promised me? Or would you prefer me to convert the wooden pot stand in the kitchen into firewood while you're out?'

I laughed out loud, as Cindy got up and stretched. Just at that, I heard Nan coming into the kitchen, the laborious clump-clump-clump-clump of her walking sticks giving the game away very easily.

'I'll need to get going, Ian,' she said wearily, the big dark circles under her eyes revealing the physical and emotional struggle that she was now facing every single day of her young life. 'Can you put my shoes on for me and help me into the car?'

'Sure,' I said, as I rose to my feet, 'And when do you want me to pick you up tonight?'

'Oh, let's just wait and see how I get on at school this morning, can we? The way I'm feeling right now, I don't know if I'll even make it to lunch time.' My heart sank.

The almost daily deterioration in Nan's condition was spectacular, if extremely depressing to behold. This time last month, she was still managing to walk to school, which was located only about 400 metres from our front door, although the term 'walking' was a bit of a misnomer even at that stage. Shuffling along at a bloody snail's pace while hanging onto two walking sticks for dear life, would have been a much more accurate description. Today, though, she couldn't even get as far as our front gate, without hanging onto my arm as if her very life depended on it. It was hellish to witness, simply hellish.

'And what were Cindy and you talking about?' she enquired once she had reached the temporary respite of the car's passenger seat, trying to force a little artificial smile, but kidding neither of us.

'Oh, we were just saying that we're going to invent *Cindy Power* to help you to get better,' I replied.

'Nothing will help me now, Ian,' she said wearily, 'I'm not going to get any better, am I?'

'Well, Cindy thinks you are, don't you Cindy? And she says that the four of us are all going to get through this.'

'The four of us?' Nan asked with a puzzled expression.

'Yup. You, me, Cindy and our new wee girl,' I replied. 'Cindy wants us to call her Bessie!'

'Oh, so it's to be a wee girl then, has it? And Bessie?' Nan asked. 'Wee Bessie McMurdo! Aye, that'll be right. Why Bessie, for goodness sake?'

'Because that was Cindy's mother's name,' I said.

Nan let out a big laugh, which soothed my soul and warmed my heart. 'How on earth did you know that "Bessie" was Cindy's mother's name, Ian?' she asked.

And I replied, 'Do you know something? I've got no idea. Not a bloody clue!'

Just at that, Cindy turned towards me, and opened her mouth ever so slightly but just enough to reveal that familiar tongue again. She raised her right eyebrow. She was smiling at me again. Her eyes twinkled like distant stars in a neon-free evening sky.

I could have sworn that she winked at me.

The Sixth Sense

'The more enlightened our houses are, the more their walls ooze ghosts.'
(Italo Calvino, The Literature Machine)

The strange art of *Cindy Power* was to manifest itself on many occasions over the months and years ahead, invariably through what our behavioural hypnotist friends might refer to as 'subliminal messages', and sometimes in quite spectacular fashion. However, and given that any form of communication requires both a sender and receiver of the message in question, whether it be a phone call, discussion, or some weird 'connection' between a couple of sensitised souls, I invariably found myself reflecting on whether this particular phenomenon was the exclusive domain of Cindy and myself. If it was, then might it be the case that I was simply imagining everything, that the subliminal messages between us were merely figments of an imagination that was once described by a former headmaster as the most vivid he had ever known?

If so, that would account for my enforced invention of the ethereal Meg in my supercharged early teens. It would explain my trance in the car. Indeed, it would rationalise many things and, as a supposed scientist, God knows my connection with Cindy was crying out for some kind of convincing rationalisation. However, it would also render many aspects of my desktop research inconclusive and, worse still, the very notion of *Cindy Power* and even *Dogmanese* itself as cartloads of claptrap.

Most importantly though, and just as I had done all these years ago with my imaginary Meg, I knew I desperately needed this connection with Cindy to be 'real' and sustainable. After all, she was fast becoming my main source of inspiration, my deeply trusted friend, my counsellor, my rock. All of which, of course, was fine and well but simply persuaded my scientific brain that my belief in the special connection between Cindy and me was being influenced in large measure, and perhaps even exclusively, by my overwhelming need for its very existence. I didn't like that particular thought, not one little bit.

I had spoken to Nan about *Cindy Power* on quite a number of occasions and together we had begun to pretend that some kind of inexplicable force was at play, this able to fend off many of the demons that she was facing, in a metaphysical 'Popeye-The-Sailor-Man-With-Dog-Biscuits-Instead-Of-Spinach' kind of way. Quite often the technique worked, and it got us through many a potentially depressing situation, but in Nan's view it was nothing more and nothing less than that. A technique, end of story.

By way of illustration, one day the three of us were walking from a local car park towards the doctors' surgery where Nan had yet another appointment with her own GP, this time to see about whether she could be referred to a counsellor to help her to deal with the depression that had been hanging over her recently, like a huge black cloud.

Picture the scene, if you will, Nan shuffling one laborious step at a time with her legs trembling uncontrollably, her right hand on a walking stick and her left hand grabbing my right forearm as if her very life depended on it, an almost-full-term baby in her tummy and my left hand holding onto Cindy's straining leash. It was a pretty common scene in those days, but one that must have filled the local townsfolk with roughly equal doses of deep sympathy and huge amusement. It really must have resembled a wicked scene from a *National Lampoon's* send-up movie, and we still laugh to this day when we think about it.

However, the apparition was about to get even more surreal for any nosey bastards who just happened to be peeking naughtily from behind their psychedelic-seventies curtains. Somehow, Nan managed to put her walking stick down one of the slats in a drain cover, rather than onto the pavement, and down she went. She began to fall slowly at first, in fact quite gracefully as I recall. I grabbed her arm and managed to hold her in position for a few moments, at an angle of about forty-five degrees, thus thankfully preventing her crashing onto the road and hurting either herself or our new baby. Okay smart arse, what's your next move, I thought. Then it came to me in a flash of pure inspiration.

'Right Nan, don't panic, you'll be okay. We're going to use .... Toot-Ta-Toot-Ta-Toot-Ta-Toot .... *Cindy Power!*'

Then, somehow, I contrived to haul her back onto her unsteady feet, by sheer brute force, while pretending that it was actually Cindy herself who was carrying out the rescue procedure. Considering the predicament we had found ourselves in, perhaps it had been. Nan was most impressed, and we later enjoyed a good laugh at the whole thing.

On many occasions, particularly when Nan was feeling really down or when we simply couldn't see the positive side of a particular situation, we would enlist *Cindy Power*, normally heralded by the Toot-Ta-Toot-Ta-Toot-Ta-Toot trumpet call. Sometimes it worked and sometimes it didn't. It all depended on the seriousness of the situation, but even more importantly, on Nan's frame of mind at the time.

However, this type of thing wasn't the real *Cindy Power* that I had come to recognise on a personal level, and to be able call upon in my own times of need. Far from it, that particular phenomenon involved a very spiritual and much more profound connection between Cindy and me, something that really did present as having considerable *gravitas*. I often wondered if that special connection, real or imagined, would remain exclusively between the two of us for eternity, or if anyone else would ever share the privilege. One morning in May, I was to find out.

Nan's beloved dad, Arthur, had not kept good health for a number of years and, on top of it all, he had just suffered a massive stroke. The old man had tragically passed away early the previous morning. I took the phone call from the hospital ward sister at 6.15 a.m. and it fell to me to break the sad news to Nan, and also to her mum Jean who had been staying with us during Arthur's final days in hospital. They were both heartbroken.

The next morning, a very strange thing happened. As Nan and I were lying in bed, the phone rang. I jumped up and looked at my watch. It was 6.15 a.m. Again.

'Holy shit, that's weird,' I said to Nan.

'What is?' she asked wearily.

'Do you hear the phone ringing?' I said.

She nodded her head and said sleepily, 'I wonder who it is at this time of the morning?'

I added, 'It's quarter-past-six. That's exactly the same time as we got the phone call yesterday morning, isn't it?' Nan, still half-sleeping, nodded again.

I got out of bed, slipped on my denims and a T-shirt and trudged in the direction of the staircase to answer the phone, which hung on the kitchen wall downstairs and was still ringing. As soon as I opened the bedroom door, the ringing stopped.

As I went into the upstairs hallway, I could see that there was a light on in the kitchen. Given that the kitchen doubled as Cindy's bedroom, I was a bit puzzled, because any time we had previously left the kitchen light switched on inadvertently, that would normally have been the welcome signal for her to wander upstairs and deposit herself outside our bedroom door. However, on this occasion, Cindy was nowhere to be seen. As soon as I started walking down the stairs, I could hear someone speaking. I sat on the middle landing of the staircase and just listened for a few minutes.

A conversation was taking place. A conversation with only one voice. Very strange, I thought.

I walked into the kitchen, and there was Jean sitting at the table, her eyes swollen and red. Sitting opposite her, and perched regally on another kitchen chair, was Cindy.

'Did I hear you talking to someone there, Jean,' I asked.

'Yes you did,' she replied. 'Cindy and I were just having a wee blether, weren't we Cindy? That's a clever big dog you've got there, Ian.'

I forced an amused laugh, but one that had its roots more in intrigue than in amusement *per se*.

'So what were you two blethering about then?' I enquired rhetorically, while casting an inquisitive glance towards Cindy's intelligent face and big wide-awake eyes.

Her tail gave a couple of flicks. 'And you shouldn't be up on that chair, now should you Cindy?' She blinked once or twice, and smacked her lips. Her eyes beseeched me not to put her down onto the cold floor tiles.

Jean sighed a heavy, weary sigh and said, 'I was just telling Cindy all about Arthur, and how he had looked after me for so many years.' The enormity of the old man's passing hit home again. Nan and her mum really could have done without this. There again, so too could the dear old man himself.

'And what was Cindy saying to you?' I enquired naughtily.

'Oh, just that I would miss him, but that things would work out fine,' she replied.

'And what other little gems of wisdom did she tell you, Jean?' I teased both of them, while looking at Cindy.

She too looked at Cindy then replied, 'You told me quite a lot, didn't you Cindy? You said that I would soon have a beautiful little granddaughter, and that she would be a very special little girl indeed.'

I caught my breath.

Cindy looked straight at me, with her mouth slightly open and the pinkness of her tongue just visible over her gleaming white incisors. Ever so slightly, she raised her right eyebrow. It's a funny thing, but I didn't feel unnerved or spooked in the slightest by what Jean had said. At least, not until the next bit of the conversation took place.

'I hope I didn't disturb the two of you, then. It was just the phone ringing that woke me,' I said. 'Did you answer it? Who was it?'

Jean looked at me with a rather puzzled expression and replied, 'Ian, I've been sitting here with Cindy since three o'clock this morning, and the phone hasn't rung at all. Not once.'

That one did spook me, and a shiver ran up my spine. However, the telephone mystery was about to deepen still further.

In those days, there was no automatic 'last-number-dialled' or any such electronic recall facility on the British telephone system, so I really had no way of knowing who had called, if indeed anyone had, other than to call the operator which I was simply too knackered to do at such an unearthly hour of the morning. So I let it go, and went back to bed to find Nan still fast asleep.

However, at precisely six-fifteen the very next morning, exactly the same thing happened. And the next again. Very weird indeed, I remember thinking.

On each occasion, Nan and I had clearly heard the phone ringing, but when I got up out of bed it had stopped. Furthermore Nan's mum, who had been sleeping in the downstairs bedroom adjacent to the kitchen, had again heard nothing. Not a single thing. Very strange, we both thought, and a wee bit spooky into the bargain. So immediately after the final early morning telephone episode, I decided to call the operator. By this time it was almost six-thirty.

When I lifted the handset and put it to my ear, there was a strange 'click-click-click' sound, and a steady but very light 'buzzing' background noise from the earpiece.

'Curiouser and curiouser', I thought aloud, paraphrasing Lewis Carroll's immortal line to keep my spirits up.

I then dialled the operator. Strangely, there was no ring tone, but a female voice replied almost immediately.

'YES?'

The suddenness of the reply, and the impersonal, brusque tone of the sharp voice on the other end of the line really startled me.

'Who .... who is this?' I stammered.

'Customer Call-Back!' snapped the same voice.

'Oh ………… I'm sorry ………….. I wonder if you could tell me who dialled this number a few minutes ago?' I enquired a tad hesitantly.

A pause, then the strange voice replied, 'Just trying to connect you.'

I waited for a few minutes. Then for a few more.

I spoke again into the mouthpiece, 'Hello?'

'Just trying to connect you.'

Again I waited. And waited.

'Hello?' I said once more.

'Just trying to connect you.'

I continued to wait, until I eventually noticed that the big clock on the kitchen wall was informing me that I had been hanging on the phone for almost twenty minutes by then. I also noticed that the early morning sun's rays had begun to cast long shadows over the kitchen furniture, magnifying their sizes and distorting their shapes like ghastly props in a Hammer horror movie.

So again I whispered gently down the phone, trying my best not to wake Nan and Jean, 'Hello, is there………?'

And a lady shrieked at the pitch of her voice, 'I TOLD YOU I'M JUST F - - -ING TRYING TO CONNECT YOU!!!'

I staggered backwards and dropped the phone on the floor. I completely froze, and stared in astonishment at Cindy. Her body was lowered, her hackles raised and her top lip curled over her teeth. A very low continuous growl came unwillingly from her mouth as she glowered at the handset lying on the kitchen floor. I pulled the phone connection out of the wall socket.

I marched through to the living room, with Cindy in hot pursuit, and switched on the television. The two of us just sat there, doing nothing and saying very little for the best part of an hour, until I plucked up enough courage to go back through and re-connect the phone, then call the operator again. My heart was pounding, not out of fear of any physical harm, but out of irrational dread of some malevolent force in the ether.

This time there was no 'click-click-clicking', no 'buzzing' and the friendly, welcoming voice just said, 'Hello, operator. Can I help you?'

I told her what had happened, the whole story. She listened carefully, then asked me to repeat what the previous operator had said when she first took my call.

'Customer Call-Back,' I reminded her.

And she replied, 'Mr McMurdo, there is no such thing as Customer Call-Back.'

As I looked at Cindy, her hackles were still raised, her top lip still quivering up and down across her teeth. Her low, very serious growl continued to disturb the early-morning silence.

To this day, I have absolutely no rational explanation to offer as to what really happened on that particular morning. In no way could I even begin to explain the weird sequence of events that had just taken place. All I can offer by way of possible explanation is that the house seemed to be full of blisteringly high energy and emotion that day, so much so that I could almost taste them.

I can tell you one thing for sure, though. Cindy knew an awful lot more about it than I did.

The Day The Penny Dropped

*'Do not dwell in the past, do not dream of the future,
concentrate the mind on the present moment.'*
(Buddha)

Arthur was laid to rest on the twenty-eighth of May, the same date as my dear old Papa had died several years back, and yet the same as that on which Nan's mum would be cremated some three decades later. One day soon, I really must try to develop a huge psychological complex about that particular date, because it also happens to be my own birthday. Just think of the money it would save my family and friends, if instead of yet again having to fund my eagle-eyed anticipation of assorted presents, they might instead only require to visit me in an institution for the chronically dribbling-and-twitching. One has to be pragmatic about such things, you know.

It's a strange thing, but amid all the various health problems, heartaches and numerous other setbacks that we had required to face within our first couple of years of marriage, I was actually by this time becoming slightly more confident about our future as a family. Nan did, of course, have to bear the brunt of the pressure, since it was her father who had recently passed away, not mine, and it was she who was facing a lifetime of chronic disability, not me.

However, it was my job to steer us all through the rough-and-tough times that lay ahead, or 'lead' us through them as Cindy had somehow managed to counsel me. I also knew for certain that it was the bizarre connection with my big manic mutt that was responsible for these new and increasing waves of hope and optimism that were beginning to wash over my weary soul.

I soon found that I could turn to Cindy on a regular and even routine basis, and deploy her as a conveniently silent receptacle for my anxiety-ridden tales of woe, almost always emerging from our various discussions feeling supremely confident that not only had she listened to my ramblings, but that she had actually understood them into the bargain. The fact of the matter was that Cindy was fast becoming my very first port of call when I needed to get something off my chest. It wasn't the case that I couldn't speak to Nan, it was just that she had quite enough on her plate already, without needing to be burdened by someone who should be demonstrating strong and purposeful leadership, rather than deep and pathetic insecurity.

What was even more remarkable was that every time I spoke to Cindy, she would just sit there, seemingly hanging onto my every despairing word. Whether she actually understood all, or even any of it, I will never really know for sure, but she certainly appeared to recognise exactly what I was droning on about.

In my times of need – and, believe me, there were many around that time - there was deep concentration in her big bright eyes, complete stillness in her posture and intense love in her heart. Most times, the aftermath of our discussions would find me in a much more enlightened frame of mind and very often with a renewed sense of direction and purpose. Without a single exception, I would always feel happier, more relaxed and less anxious about the future.

I even tried little experiments with her, to test out our range of 'discussion topics'. I spoke to her about football. I asked her about horse racing. I ranted and raved about our obnoxious near-neighbour who kept parking his bloody van across our driveway. I asked her for the weather forecast. I tried out a few jokes with her, and even attempted to rehearse a few after-dinner speeches that I had written for the local Burns Supper 'circuit', to which I had been persuaded to return by some crafty, but very caring mates.

Every time I tried innocuous stuff like this on her, she would yawn, stretch, fidget, scratch herself and get up and walk away, clearly bored out of her mind with the proceedings. At such times, there would invariably be little and sometimes no eye contact. She simply wasn't interested in such matters of pure trivia. It was as if the only time I could really engage on a truly emotional level with Cindy, was when I was speaking with my heart and soul.

How the hell could she do that, I often wondered? How could she actually tell the difference between things that really mattered and trivial bullshit?

I put the 'telephone incident' down to an unfortunate and misguided prank, simply because the alternative explanation was too unsettling, but I always knew intuitively that a 'sixth sense' happening had taken place under my own roof.

The big day was fast approaching, the one that would increase the size of our happy little family to three human beings and one quasi-human dog. Taking advice from the local hospital staff, I tried my very best to persuade Nan that she must try to practise her 'walking', to keep her as fit and supple as possible when the baby arrived.

Every other evening after work, I would help her into the car, while Cindy jumped into the back seat, and then drive us to a secluded spot in the countryside. There I would get Nan to stand, her hands trembling on her two walking sticks, and coax her to shuffle towards me, always remaining just close enough to catch her if she stumbled, and prevent her from falling onto the road. It was an exercise in utter hopelessness and sheer frustration, borne out of blind faith in an equally confused medical profession. On almost every single occasion, Nan would need to be half-cajoled and half-lifted back into the car, most often in tears.

On one occasion, her 'good' leg – the one that could still take her weight – completely gave way and she crashed down towards the tarmac, with yours truly just managing to break her fall before any damage was done to Nan or our unborn child. As I physically carried her back to the car, I turned my head away from her to make sure that she couldn't see the tears of deep sympathy and complete desperation that were welling up in my eyes.

As I blinked them away, I remember noticing that Cindy, who had been playing all by herself in an adjacent field, was just standing there, staring at me. Her mouth was closed, her gait was rigid and her tail was stalk-still. She was scolding me, radiating waves of scarcely-concealed displeasure. And as usual, the signals were coming from her eyes.

When we got home, Nan went for a quiet lie-down on top of the bed. She was exhausted, completely and utterly exhausted. For some strange reason, Cindy just wouldn't come near me. In fact, when I sat down on the settee, she just got up and wandered away into the kitchen, then lay down in her own bed. When I walked into the kitchen, she then rose from her bed and trudged slowly past me into the hall, where she just lay down outside the spare bedroom door.

'Okay, go in a bloody huff,' I said to her, and proceeded to make myself a sandwich. Not even the smell of food could entice Cindy back to my side. For the very first time since she had become part of our family three years back, I realised that she was really upset with me. And the thing was that I knew exactly why.

'I'M ONLY DOING WHAT THE BLOODY QUACKS ARE TELLING ME TO DO!' I shouted at her, in a voice that radiated both irritation and despair.

Cindy just turned her head in the opposite direction, put her chin down on her front paws and stared at the door of the spare bedroom, behind which Nan was lying in exhausted recuperation. I slammed the kitchen door shut, threw my half-made sandwich into the hot, soapy water in the sink and stormed out of the back door and down the steps towards the town centre, where my intended destination was to be the Royal Hotel bar, in which I would anaesthetise my aching brain with two, or even three pints of Tartan Special.

In the event, I only got to the end of the road, realised I was behaving like a bloody infant, told myself to grow up and shuffled wearily back home. When I opened the door, Cindy was standing there, wagging her tail.

'I need to talk to you,' I said to her.

'I know you do,' her big eyes replied.

And that was the day the penny dropped.

Cindy and I had already learned to speak to each other. Not in the way humans do, and not through the deployment of the Queen's English or some quaint Scottish vernacular. Instead, we had learned to communicate with each other in our own very special and very secret language, the one we called *Dogmanese*.

A language without words.

A Gift From Heaven

'Children reinvent your world for you.'
(Susan Sarandon, American Actress)

On 17 September 1976, Nan gave birth to a beautiful blue-eyed, blonde baby girl. We had previously decided that we would call our first born Alan, but the anatomical characteristics that materialised at 7.45 a.m. on that joyous Friday morning immediately put paid to such a quaint idea.

I told Cindy about the arrival of her 'wee sister' Jillian later that day, but since my dubious pronouncements were somewhat influenced by consumption of copious quantities of the *Bold John Barleycorn* by that time, she had simply yawned, scratched her ears and muttered in the secret silence of *Dogmanese*, 'Oh dear, he's pissed again.'

About a week later, the medics eventually permitted me to collect my wife and baby, and take them home. Really nice of them, don't you think? And to think that, these days, mother-and-baby get shown the door five minutes after the placenta has been removed. Just what is the world coming to?

I was really excited at the prospect of bringing my wife and baby daughter back to our home-and-castle, for two principal reasons. Firstly, I was beside myself with gleeful anticipation and wicked intrigue about how our manic mutt would take to her new charge. Secondly, I simply couldn't wait to introduce myself to the enormous breasts that Nan had developed, seemingly overnight. Allow me, if you will, to regale you on the resounding success of former, whilst sparing you a deeply depressing account of massive rejection on the latter.

Cindy was in the kitchen when we arrived back from the

maternity ward, stripping the wallpaper and sharpening the furniture as usual.

'Cindy!' I shouted, as I turned the key in the big oak door, 'Look who's here to meet you!'

Cindy thundered along the hall, her first reaction being to jump up on me, but as usual, never on Nan, whose hands she just licked frantically in joyous welcome as the new mother hobbled unsteadily on her two sticks. Cindy knew the score, don't ask me how, but she just knew. No way would she ever have done anything further to destabilise her beloved 'mummy'.

'Come and see who we've brought you, Cindy!' I said, displaying proud excitement and latent dread in roughly equal measure. 'You've got a new wee sister!'

I walked nervously into the lounge and placed the Moses basket on the couch, which was situated beneath the big bay window. Cindy made a beeline straight towards it. The moment of truth, I surmised, as I rather nervously gulped in a huge quantity of autumnal air.

Cindy put her front paws up on the couch and immediately stuck her big intelligent head straight into the basket. She stood there almost motionless for the best part of a minute sniffing gently at Jillian, starting at her head and gradually circumscribing every square centimetre of her tiny frame. No barking, no whining, no tail wagging. Nothing. Nan and I looked at each other, just managing to stifle a pair of synchronised, if very apprehensive giggles. Had she chosen to do so, Cindy could easily have devoured our new baby there and then, and in one gulp too.

She then took her paws off the couch, turned around, wandered over first to me and then to Nan, and finally trotted back over to the Moses basket once again. Up went the front paws again, and into the basket went the head. This time, after a few more intrigued sniffings, she gave Jillian's forehead the tiniest lick with her tongue. Jillian stirred slightly from her slumbers and Cindy tilted her head. And then the most welcome thing happened. She turned towards us and wagged her tail.

'Is that your new wee sister, lass?' I asked her quietly. Still standing with her front paws on the couch and her back legs on the carpet, she sniffed again and watched in fascination as Jillian stretched and squirmed to signal her transition from deep sleep into semi-consciousness. All the while, Cindy just stood there wagging her tail with increasing frequency and looking around at both of us every now and again, presumably for some form of psychological reassurance.

'Make a big fuss of the dog when you bring your baby home,' Robbie, our family vet, had counselled us.

And that we surely did. We patted her head and told her repeatedly what a good dog she was, we rubbed her belly as she rolled on the carpet, and we administered enough gravy biscuits to feed the entire and much less fortunate population of Battersea Dogs' Home. I took her out for a walk and she behaved like a six-month-old puppy, exhibiting an immaturity and hyperactivity that was quite fascinating to behold.

After half an hour or so, I asked Cindy where her new wee sister was and she just barked, and barked, and barked. When we got back in the house, she absolutely bolted into the lounge and over to the couch where Jillian had earlier lain in the relative peace of her Moses basket. However, this time the baby was nowhere to be seen. So she ran back out again and sprinted along the hallway and into the kitchen at breakneck speed, where she found Nan sitting on a chair breast-feeding the baby.

Still wagging her tail furiously, Cindy sat at Nan's feet for a few moments, trying to work out what exactly was happening to her hitherto carefully structured canine world. Eventually, she could take the intrigue no longer and let out an ear-splitting bark. Jillian jumped, immediately stopped feeding and then started bawling. Cindy's head tilted from side to side, her tail continuing to wag furiously. All the time, we clapped her head and spoke to her, telling her what a clever dog she was, and what a beautiful wee sister she had, one who would take her lots of walks and look after her when she grew up. Thankfully, it would be another twelve years before Jillian and her little brother would have their hearts broken, looking on helplessly from the top of the stairwell as Cindy lay dying in my arms one dreadful October evening.

Cindy and I had another one of our secret little chats that evening, after Nan had fed and changed the baby, and I had placed her ever-so-carefully into her brand new cot. As I sprawled out on the lounge carpet with my back against the chair, Cindy came over and sat beside me. I looked into her eyes and the whole thing started again.

I watched in complete fascination as another conversation in *Dogmanese* began, and as her pupils dilated then retracted, again and again and again, in majestic harmony with her ever-changing head position, facial expression and body posture.

'Do you like your new wee sister?'

'Yes, I like her a lot.'

'That's good. We'll have great fun as we watch her growing up. And when she's a wee bit bigger, we'll be able to run and play with her in the park.'

'But we have great fun just now,' a pair of temporarily worried eyes opined.

'I know, and that will never change.'

'Will Nan and you still like me too?'

'More than ever, you silly big dog.'

'If anybody comes near my wee sister, I'll rip their heads off.'

And from that moment forth, Jillian had acquired a personal bodyguard. Any time a visitor decided to come to the door, well-wishing and gift-bearing though he or she may have been, Cindy would position herself strategically between stranger and beloved baby. And as Jillian grew up, she would come to like the special feeling of canine protection very much indeed.

She told me many years later that it made her feel invincible.

It's A Vet's Life

'Physician, heal thyself.'
(Hebrew Proverb)

Cindy had a very clear philosophy on life. To her, its whole purpose was to have fun, and the more of it the merrier. A simple philosophy it may have been, and quite lacking in ambiguity, but completely persuasive in its implementation.

Her entire raison d'etre seemed to centre around waking up bright and early in the morning, munching on a healthy breakfast, converting every single minute of the daylight hours into riotous-but-harmless mayhem, gorging on a hearty dinner, and then crashing out in her comfy bed to recharge her batteries, in order to start the whole cyclical process all over again the following morning. It really was quite remarkable to behold.

There seemed to be no canine equivalents to pouring over the day's latest depressing news headlines, or awkward phone calls to return, or truculent work colleagues to humour, or disbelieving gasps as the latest bank statement was ripped from its envelope. Cindy's philosophy was all about the positives, while the negatives simply had no place in her life. Perhaps there are some important attitudinal lessons that we could all learn from our dogs.

Cindy loved most things about life, and those she didn't love she just liked quite a lot. Now, admittedly, she really did enjoy the proverbial 'life of Riley'. She had a very comfortable home to live in, food and water in her big plastic bowls whenever she needed them, a cosy bed to sleep in during the night, and a loving, doting family to care for her twenty-four-seven. In all honesty, and in comparison with countless millions of poor, unfortunate animals all over the world whose daily lives revolve around hunger, thirst, neglect and wanton cruelty, there was very little in Cindy's life that was not to like. Consider this though.

How many people do you know personally, who appear to have it all – and often handed to them on a plate, into the bargain – but who still manage to mope along all day with their big serious faces tripping them, as if they are carrying the weight of the world on their own shoulders? It really is quite amazing how few people these days actually come across as solution-orientated optimists, and yet how many present as woe-is-me merchants of doom. Sure, many individuals and families have a great deal on their plates in a metaphorical sense and in terms of assorted health, monetary and other quality-of-life problems, whilst having very little on their plates in the real sense of the term. However, I ask you, is it always the unfortunate souls in our increasingly self-centred societies today who are the serial pessimists, or might there just be a little paradox in there?

Whatever the answer to the above little conundrum, I do have to admit that Cindy did have it all. In fact, like a lot of dogs in this opulent land of ours, there is little doubt that she was treated and cared for much better than at least thirty-per-cent of the world's human population at the time, which is quite a sobering thought, really.

However, humanitarian and sociological dilemmas notwithstanding, my point is this. Many of us today just seem hopelessly incapable of accepting what we do have – particularly those of us who are fortunate enough to have it – and sailing through the day with a smile on our face, rather than trudging along with an expression that would turn milk sour. I should know, because I constantly have to remind myself – or be reminded – to stop mumping and moaning about the little insignificant irritations in life, and count my many blessings. Ho-hum.

So thankfully, and of course just like the vast majority of

healthy and well-cared-for dogs, Cindy was blessed with bursting energy levels, radiant positivity and an unmistakable, irrepressible *joie de vivre*. She loved life, she loved her family and she loved, well, everything really. Except for one thing, that is.

She absolutely hated the vet.

Allow me if you will, to ask you a few fairly simple questions at this point, the relevance of which might not immediately seem evident.

Have you ever seen what happens when a big blob of ice cream lands on top of a slice of searing hot apple pie? Or to the frost on your car windscreen when you spray it with a can of de-icer on a freezing-cold morning? Or do you by any chance remember your science teacher showing you the change in the colour of litmus solution when, first acid, then alkali is poured in? Or perhaps the naturally-defensive reaction of a carefree hedgehog when, all of a sudden, someone touches the poor thing?

Well, trust me, if you tend to think of the above changes as in any way spontaneous, you ought to have seen the dramatic transformation in Cindy's body language the very moment she found herself being driven into the car park outside the veterinary surgery.

Cindy absolutely, completely and utterly detested poor Robbie. And the thing is that he was such a nice guy too. But, unfortunately, as far as Cindy was concerned, he was the devil incarnate, Satan himself. And he must be destroyed.

I simply lost count of the number of discussions in *Dogmanese* that I had with Cindy on the matter, all of which started calmly and amicably enough, but the great majority of which soon disintegrated into pure canine truculence. A typical one would go something like this.

'Cindy, are your ears still itching, lass? You'll need to remember to stop putting your head under the water, because it just irritates them.'

'My ears are fine, thanks very much.' Cindy looks straight at me, mouth closing, with top and bottom sets of teeth beginning to clench slightly. She shakes her head violently to ease the itch in her ears, then remembers that she has just given the game away.

'I've cleaned them for you every morning and night for the past few days, but they don't seem to be getting any better, do they?'

'My ears are fine. Are you deaf?' Her mouth tightens, and her eyebrows go down. She glares at me, and her pupils contract. Cindy is getting annoyed.

'No, but you soon might be! I think you probably need more of these nice drops again. They certainly helped you last time.'

'Well, go and get them, then. I'll let you put them in my ears like you did last time, as long as I always get a biscuit like last time.' She raises her eyebrows, one slightly higher than the other, and her mouth begins to relax somewhat. Her pupils expand just enough for the change to be noticeable.

'But Robbie needs to take a wee swab from your ears first, so that he can tell whether it's a fungal or a bacterial infection.'

At the very mention of Robbie's name, Cindy's pupils go on full beam alert. She springs to her feet and begins grinding her teeth. Her tail is as rigid as a poker. 'I'M NOT GOING NEAR THAT BLOODY DEVIL VET AGAIN! NEVER!'

Cindy trots out of the kitchen whilst glancing sideways towards me with a deathly stare, runs along the hall and skips up the stairs, where she slumps down in the relative security of the half-landing.

It's a funny thing, you know, but every single one of my five wonderful big dogs have somehow developed a phobia about our various vets. I often wonder what the common denominator might be. However, of all of them, Cindy was the absolute limit, she really was. And the strange thing is that her veterinary paranoia began to reveal itself at a remarkably young age.

As most of you will appreciate whether you are dog owners or not, it is vitally important to have a puppy inoculated as early as possible against a whole host of potentially nasty and very infectious diseases, just the same as you would with your own baby, the only difference being that puppies are inoculated against distemper, Parvovirus and such like things, rather than measles, whooping cough and other human ailments. These days, the first injection is normally administered when the puppy is around 7 weeks' old, with the second about 5 weeks later, whereas in Cindy's day, puppies wouldn't be fully protected until they were about 4 or 5 months old.

I do actually remember taking Cindy to the vet for her puppy jags, but very little of the detail, which makes me think that the whole thing must have been pretty uneventful. However, with the benefit of hindsight, how I wish now that I had appreciated that visit much more, because from thereon in, our trips to the vet's surgery were the stuff of living nightmares.

When Cindy was just over a year old, a note dropped through our letterbox, informing us the she was now due to have her 'annual booster' injection, and so I phoned to make an appointment. In preparation for her first visit to the vet as ' a big dog now', I decided to walk her the half-mile or so down to the surgery, doing a slight detour into the local park *en route*, in order that she would be both exercised and relaxed. She would soon transpire to be very exercised indeed, but not in the way I had planned, and most certainly not relaxed in the slightest.

As soon as I got to within twenty metres of the surgery, Cindy simply put the brakes on. A team of wild horses couldn't have shifted her. There was nothing else for it, so I physically picked her up and carried her into the building, while she wriggled and squirmed and kicked and panted like a teenage child possessed by Satan. It really was a hellish performance for a one-year-old dog.

As we sat in the waiting room, with Cindy shaking and quivering and trying to clamber up onto my knee, everyone just stared. Not at Cindy, but at me of course.

'Come in, Cindy! And let's have a wee look at you!' came the friendly, booming welcome from Robbie, as he stood there smiling confidently, all kitted out in his pristine medical overalls.

Cindy immediately scrambled right under the seat, so far underneath in fact that only the whites of her eyes could still be seen. Robbie, his receptionist and I then tried everything to get her to come back out, even tempting her with a selection of dog biscuits and a half-eaten *Mars Bar*, but she was for none of it. Eventually, I had no option but to simply haul on her leash and physically drag her out, as she slithered along the tiled floor on her belly, with her claws desperately trying to get some purchase. It really was most embarrassing.

'Pop her on the scales, Ian,' said Robbie nonchalantly, 'so that we can tell how her weight is doing.'

I just carried Cindy over to the other side of the room and put her on the scales, which had a big rubber mat custom-designed for animals to sit on, and then I commanded her to 'sit'. She just flumped down in a heap, as if she was dead.

I lifted her up again, shoved her backside down on the mat, and said in a determined voice, 'SIT!' Down she went once again, dead as the proverbial dodo. Three times more I repeated the whole procedure, and on each increasingly infuriating occasion she collapsed in an inanimate heap.

By this time, the other people in the waiting room were starting to giggle and my face was becoming increasingly scarlet. Even their assorted pets were gawking in disbelief at the little bastard's truculence. After about the fifth or sixth attempt, Robbie decided to come over and assist, at which point the 'corpse' immediately took wings and bolted straight for the surgery door, knocking over a display stand and causing every single animal in the premises to make its own barking, howling, mewing, hissing and squawking contribution towards the loudest cacophony of noise I had ever witnessed in my twenty-five years. It was sheer bloody mayhem.

We had no option but to give up on the weighing-in notion and, on Robbie's advice, I again carried Cindy this time into his consultation room, where I did as he requested and lifted her onto the examination table. She hit the deck again like a sack of potatoes, only this time shivering and shaking like a Californian beach babe in a Siberian winter. Robbie did his best to give Cindy her annual health check, as she lay there grunting and grimacing and growling like petrified child in a pitiful strop.

However, it was when the syringe came out that the situation escalated from amber to red alert. As soon as Robbie squirted a few excess drops of clear liquid from the top of the needle, to expel any unwanted bubbles of air, Cindy sprang back to life, leapt off the table and onto the floor, where she fairly skidded into the far wall with a resounding 'thump'. Having reached the limit of my exasperation levels by that time, I just pounced on her like a rugby player in a vicious scrum, and pinned her to the floor with her backside sticking outwards.

'Hold her there, Ian,' Robbie shouted, and plunged the needle into her exposed arse, at which point Cindy let out an almighty 'H-O-O-O-O-W-W-W-W-L', and pissed all over my shoes.

'See you next year, Cindy!' Robbie said cheerily, as I carried my loveable basket-case out the surgery door.

'Not if I see you first!' hissed Cindy, through so many of her gleaming-white incisors that I went momentarily blind.

I took Cindy home and told Nan the tale as she was serving dinner. I seem to recall that she eventually stopped laughing just before *News At Ten* started. Unfortunately, that day's veterinary incident was by no means untypical, in terms of Cindy's behaviour in the surgery. Indeed, on at least three or four future occasions, she even managed to eclipse that particular performance-from-hell, if you can actually believe such a thing possible.

The visits to the vet always seemed to follow an amazingly similar pattern.

Step 1
A prior discussion in *Dogmanese*, between Cindy and me, that started reasonably well, but deteriorated rapidly as soon as Robbie's name was even mentioned.
Step 2
A car journey which began in near-silence, culminating in

Cindy howling and yelping and trying to wriggle under the driver's seat as soon as she got within spitting distance of the surgery. (Did you ever see the scene from the original *The Omen* film where the little boy, who has been possessed by Satan, slowly but surely loses the plot as his father's car gets closer and closer to the church? Well, that was what it was like when Cindy was getting nearer and nearer the vet's surgery, only at least ten times worse.)

Step 3

Cindy playing 'dead', and having to be carried like a bag of cement into the surgery, where she would sit in the waiting room shaking like a tin hut in an earthquake.

Step 4

Robbie appearing, and Cindy diving for cover, only to be physically dragged into his room howling and whimpering.

Step 5

An all-in wrestling match on the floor for about fifteen minutes, which would normally end with Robbie eventually managing to perform the requisite medical treatment, but only after he and I had been covered from head to toe in huge scratches and canine urine.

Step 6

Cindy dragging me frantically out of the surgery door, rasping and snarling at Robbie as the poor man said his remarkably polite goodbyes.

'Ian, please don't ever tell me in advance when she's coming in,' Robbie once famously beseeched me. 'Just phone down in the morning, and turn up later that same day. Honestly, if I knew the night before that Cindy was on the list, I wouldn't sleep a bloody wink.'

And so it went on and on and on. Every year, she had to have her annual medical check and booster injection, where she would invariably perform like a dog possessed. Occasionally, she would need to have her nails clipped, which also made her behave and howl so manically that the poor souls sitting in the waiting room must have thought she was being murdered, a dark thought that would surely have crossed Robbie's mind at least once or twice. Because Cindy spent so much time with her head submerged underneath rivers, lakes and oceans in search of assorted sunken clap-trap, she often had to have her ears cleaned out, a procedure that ended up like a battle scene from *Apocalypse Now*. And I couldn't even bring myself to tell you of the sheer carnage in the surgery whenever poor Robbie had to clear Cindy's blocked anal glands by shoving his fingers you-know-where. Let's just say that it did not whet one's appetite for dinner.

These are only a few of the blood-curdling spats that will be etched on my memory, and no doubt on Robbie's, for eternity. The strange thing was that for some reason, Cindy always knew intuitively when she was due to visit the vet, and this 'sixth sense' gift of hers would inevitably contrive to compel her to work herself into the mother-and-father of all lathers. However, there was just one little thing that Cindy's amazing psychic powers had not yet allowed her to foresee.

One day soon, it would be the devil-vet himself who would save her life.

A Tale Of Two Tails

*'Jealousy lives upon doubts. It becomes madness, or ceases entirely
as soon as we pass from doubt to certainty.'*
(Francois de la Rochefoucauld, French Author)

By this time, and through increasing mastery of our secret little language of *Dogmanese*, I had developed the uncanny knack of being able to read Cindy like the proverbial book. Okay it may well have been, and probably was, more akin to a child's first nursery book than a brilliant philosophical thesis on the emergence of existentialism in a pluralist society, but at least it was ours and nobody else's.

Wishful thinking or not, I felt that I had developed a very close bond with Cindy, and even more importantly, the art of communicating with her in an increasingly routine, but strangely reassuring fashion. Now admittedly, most dog owners can tell intuitively when their canine charges are happy or sad, relaxed or anxious, hungry or satisfied and angry or at peace with the world. However, our connection seemed to go much, much deeper than that. I often felt that I could tell what Cindy was actually thinking, and I was absolutely convinced that she could read my own thoughts pretty accurately as well.

A few days after Jillian had become the latest and exceedingly welcome addition to our little family, I had been out walking with Cindy in Woodroad Park, a large sprawling public park in Cumnock, that in those halcyon days of the late 'seventies, played host to caravans, tennis courts, children's amusements, a putting green and even an outdoor swimming pool, would you believe?

Many a terrifying childhood memory I have of being forced by our sergeant-major-like physical education teacher to jump into the freezing waters of that blasted pool, under the dubious auspices of 'swimming lessons', only to emerge in a highly traumatised and near-hypothermic state from what seemed like several hours' enforced immersion. We were timetabled for swimming at eleven o'clock on a Monday morning and it would often be well after lunchtime before the sensation eventually returned to our adolescent extremities, eagerly developing genitalia included.

So as Cindy and I meandered up the winding footpath of Woodroad Park and into the woods as usual, I let her off her leash, also as usual. However, not everything was 'as usual' on that particular occasion, because rather than sprint off at great velocity into the foliage in forlorn pursuit of hopelessly disorientated rabbits, hares, mice and anything that moved, for some odd reason Cindy just stayed welded to my side as I marched up the hill track. Very strange, I thought. So I wandered into the long grass, found a big stick and heaved it into the ferns.

'Fetch!' I shouted.

As the stick flew through the air and landed in the long stuff with an instantly recognisable 'S-W-I-I-I-S-S-S-H, Cindy just stood there like a glum party pooper. A big worried face looked up at me. It was pathetic, really.

'What's wrong, lass?' I asked, and sat down on a tree stump. She slumped down beside me, her head stretched out on her front paws, her eyebrows gathered together in anxiety. She didn't even look at me. Her tail was completely invisible beneath her prostrate frame.

'You're in the huff, aren't you?' I enquired. 'Okay, what have I done?'

Without even moving her head, she rolled her eyes sideways in my direction. The expression was a definite glower, no doubt about it.

I laughed out loud and said, 'Come on you big dope, what have I done?' At that point, Cindy let out an enormous sigh, got up and wandered a few feet away, where she slumped back down again, staring in the opposite direction.

'Oh dear,' I said, 'If you're not going to tell me what I've done, how can I possibly sort it?'

No response, neither sound-related nor even non-verbal. So I got up and walked on. Most reluctantly, she eventually got up and trudged slowly in my pursuit, but quite deliberately well behind me. However, I had also started to notice something quite different about her body language. It was something about her tail.

You see, Cindy had the waggiest tail that you could possibly imagine. Every time we spoke to her or greeted her first thing in the morning or shouted her name when we arrived back in the house, her tail would wag furiously from side-to-side. And it would wag in such an ecstatically manic fashion as to leave us in no doubt that she was beside herself with pure joy, just to see us again, and to be blessed with our company.

That particular day, though, Cindy's tail wasn't wagging at all. Something rather odd was afoot.

You see, whenever Cindy was happy, she would invariably wag her tail. Personally, I find Labradors' tails particularly easy to 'read', mainly because of their big bushy shapes, whereas I'm never quite so confident about the signals being radiated from the tails of certain smaller dog breeds, like the Jack Russell or the Yorkshire Terrier.

Sometimes Cindy appeared so elated with life that she would wag her tail so vociferously from side-to-side in an almost horizontal plane, that her entire back end would have no option but to follow suit. It really was a case of the tail wagging the dog. I always found this to be a sign that was quite impossible to misinterpret, since it clearly meant that she was just so grateful to be together with her lord-and-master, and so deliriously happy with her lot.

However on that particular occasion, Cindy's proverbial rattle had been well-and-truly flung out of the similarly proverbial pram. I already knew from my earlier reading that dogs routinely use the art of tail wagging as a very powerful means of communication. Indeed, a dog's tail can often tell you a great deal about its emotional state and psychological well-being.

Cindy's tail always seemed to serve two completely different purposes, in addition to its amazing ability to send my well-earned glass of chilled beer cascading over my new denims. First of all, she always used it very skilfully to 'steer' herself around sharp corners, as a kind of counterbalance to her normally devastating momentum, which in turn derived from the blistering speeds with which she invariably bolted from one location to another. Many a potentially disastrous collision was avoided at the very last minute, simply because of the importance of her 'rudder', namely her big bushy tail, as it contrived to drag her entire torso around a right-angled bend at near-supersonic speed.

However, her tail's other principal function was undoubtedly to assist her in the vitally important process of non-verbal communication and, through close observation, I had already built up a pretty decent understanding of the vital signs. Cindy's tail could really tell a thousand tales, if you will pardon the awful pun.

For example, when her tail was horizontal but relaxed, it signalled to me a state of mental alertness or keen attention. When horizontal but rigid, however, she was normally trying to assert her dominance or her position in the pecking order, to whoever or whatever happened to be in the vicinity at the time. If she held her tail rigid and slightly upwards, then look out Fido, because she was usually making a pretty clear statement that she was perfectly willing to justify her dominance. However, when her tail was manacled to her backside, Cindy was normally signalling that she was either feeling unwell or not particularly happy with life at the time. On the very few occasions that it was actually tucked between her hind legs, I just knew that she was really worried about something.

So there you have it, the tail is a truly wonderful thing, and especially when you are scratching your head trying to work out what your big dog is thinking, or perhaps how it is feeling.

Indeed, I often reflect that it would have been fantastic in my own formative years, if the opposite sex had been kitted out with tails. Just think of the wasted time that could have been saved in getting wee Nancy into the sack, whilst avoiding the humiliation of public rejection from big Nelly. Anyway, to the Woodroad Park story we must again return.

Thus, armed with this additional wealth of appendage-related knowledge, I attempted to place an intelligent interpretation on what had been wrong with Cindy on that particular day. It was very simple, really. She was worried about something, in a bit of a canine strop and anxious to let me know how she was feeling. It had to be about the baby, or more accurately about the new dynamics in play on account of Jillian's glorious arrival and increasing influence on the domestic scene. So when I got home, I decided to carry out a little experiment.

I took the baby through to the kitchen, and handed her to Nan. I then sat down on my favourite big chair in the lounge and shouted Cindy over to me. She came to me quite willingly, although her tail was still only flicking rather feebly and she looked as though she had just lost a hundred quid on a photo-finish. However, she did sit quite contentedly by my side as I stroked her head, and within a matter of minutes she toddled over to the other side of the room, picked up her favourite squeaky toy and brought it back over to me. I threw it out into the hall and she bolted out after it, retrieving it and dropping it at my feet.

The tail began to wag again. I threw the toy to the other side of the lounge and again she ran after it excitedly, her tail starting to swing more furiously. We played like this for a few minutes, then she started panting and barking for more, with her head lowered to the floor, her backside up in the air and her tail going like the clappers. The fun was back again. Next, I grabbed her and rolled her over on her back, rubbing her belly. Her tail swished like car windscreen wipers in a freak rainstorm. Then she bolted manically out the door, along the hall, back into the lounge again and repeated the whole procedure another three or four times, until she eventually collapsed in a heap at my feet.

'For goodness sake, what's going on through there?' shouted Nan, laughing at the sudden transformation in Cindy's mood.

'Watch this,' I said to her. I went over to Jillian's pram, spoke softly to my new daughter, then picked her up in my arms. Almost immediately, Cindy's ears pinned themselves back and she trundled out of the room with her head lowered and her tail once again welded between her back legs. She then moped past Nan without even looking up, and slumped wearily into her bed.

'That's amazing!' I exclaimed. 'The wee devil's in the huff because she's jealous of Jillian!'

'Well, she's maybe not actually jealous of her,' replied Nan. 'Maybe she's just worried that you don't have the same time for her now that the baby has come along. To be fair, you've been spending a lot of your time with Jillian recently, and probably a lot less with Cindy. So maybe she's worried that her relationship with you is going to change now that there's another star in the house.'

'Do you think so?' I asked. 'Do you really think Cindy's feelings are as profound as that?'

Nan giggled and said, 'Yes, and you know it too, Ian! She's as bright as a button, that one. You're going to have to do a bit of remedial work with your big precious dog!'

She was dead right, of course. Unwittingly, and I suppose understandably in the circumstances, I had found myself spending increasingly large chunks of time with our new baby, and therefore I suppose, to the psychological detriment of my big canine soulmate. It was a situation that had just sneaked up on me, and it was time for me to redress that particular balance.

However, it was also time for something else too. And that was for Cindy to put her hitherto impressive libido to more practical use, and learn a bit more about parenthood herself.

In other words, it was time to get her knocked up.

Al Fresco Love

'No matter how much cats fight, there always seem to be plenty of kittens.'
(Abraham Lincoln, 16th President of the United States)

Over the next few weeks and months, I really did try to spend as much time as I could with Cindy, at least insofar as my new parental responsibilities would permit from a purely practical standpoint. By no stretch of the imagination was this a hardship, though. I simply loved our time together, and she did too. For some reason, I always felt at peace with the world when the two of us were out trekking in the woods, or simply sitting side-by-side in the kitchen. Whenever I was reading the paper, she would snuggle up at my feet. If I dozed off in the chair for a few minutes, she would never be more than half a metre from my side. If for some reason I closed a door between us, she would be welded to the other side of it, waiting for me to turn the handle.

'That dog thinks the sun shines out of your backside', my beloved often informed me, partly in amused envy, but mostly in envious amusement. Cindy and I were the business, no more and no less.

By this time, Cindy was just over four years old, fully grown and worldly wise in a distinctly canine, if oddly quasi-human sense too. Whenever she sat in the lounge observing the family dynamics, or on the top step surveying the back garden that was her own personal territory, she had an air of complete superiority about her, indeed of undiluted arrogance at times. Cindy was a very confident big dog, with assuredness and surefootedness radiating unfailingly from her magnificent golden face.

When she was in one of her 'Queen of Sheba' postures, as Nan and I used to call it, I would observe Cindy's body language from a safe distance. The range of involuntary movements and ever-changing expressions she displayed within a five-minute spell was simply incredible. One moment she would be sitting and staring straight ahead in deep concentration, and the next her nose would twitch and her head would jerk from side to side, up and down. Her eyebrows would rise and fall, over and over and over again, and her pupils would dilate and contract with bewildering rapidity.

On the other hand, if Cindy caught me staring at her, she would demonstrate her mild annoyance by deploying her amazing capacity to stare straight back at me with a facial expression that said, 'And who the hell do you think you're looking at?'

I believed Cindy to be the brightest creature on God's earth, and had it not been for her abysmal handwriting, I'm convinced that she could effortlessly have completed *The Times* crossword each morning before breakfast.

Mercifully, she had developed only one of her master's three principal vices. On not one occasion, not even in a rare moment of uncontrolled exuberance, did she show even the slightest inclination to participate in the consumption of alcohol, or even gambling for that matter. However, as the good lord is my witness, she always did demonstrate a very keen interest in the time-honoured art of rumpy-pumpy.

Cindy, albeit virginal at four, always seemed to us to be a bit sex-mad, as evidenced by her frequent and ultra-embarrassing attempts to 'mount' everything that was, or presented itself as another dog's hind quarters. Indeed, such was her near-omnipresent state of lust, that it was known for her to mount human legs, feline heads and even an impressively wide range of completely inanimate objects such as soft toys, burst footballs and garden plants (excluding the thorny ones though, the attempted humping of one of which taught her a lesson she would never forget). Indeed, on one memorable occasion, she actually attempted to make love with our bank manager's leg, within minutes of him entering the living room clad in his new pin-striped suit. It really was most embarrassing.

Thus, armed with a range of deluded notions about why dogs actually mount other dogs and assorted objects, dead or alive, Nan and I resolved to put Cindy's keen interest in matters sexual, to reproductively constructive and financially rewarding use. In other words, we decided to have her mated. Or indeed, to put it in the Cumnock vernacular, we got her knocked up.

Fifty quid it cost me. This was my very first, and to my considerable credit, only involvement in the seedy world of prostitution. Fifty smackers seemed a colossal amount of money 'way back in 1977, but to be fair, we did get to watch. Suffice to say that it wasn't a particularly stimulating experience for Nan and me, although both dogs certainly seemed to enjoy it.

For the record, the nuptial act essentially distilled down to seven distinct phases:

1. Extremely awkward introductions between the two respective *Homo Sapien* couples, one summer's evening in a bungalow near Fenwick, Ayrshire
2. Manic introductions in the back garden between the two Golden Labrador would-be-lovers, one in heat and the other beside himself in lust
3. A period of increasingly frantic excitement between the pair, with both demonstrating intense enthusiasm for the sexual act, but neither having the foggiest idea about what to do to commence the process
4. An excruciating, but entirely necessary combined exercise between both male *Homo Sapiens*, involving me holding Cindy completely still while he lifted the sire-to-be onto her rear end, as our respective spouses sipped coffee in the kitchen and discussed the escalating price of soap powder and free-range eggs
5. Two-point-five seconds of frantic humping (which my wife later informed everyone present to have been 'rather impressive in relative terms', whatever she meant by that)

6. Three-and-a-half hours of howling as the successful sire attempted in vain, cigarette in mouth, to extract his willy from my poor little no-longer-virginal Cindy
7. The transaction, which rendered me fifty notes the poorer, and the male human pimp similarly the richer.

The fact of the matter is that we were extremely fortunate for the sex act to have taken place at all. You see, contrary to popular belief, dogs do not actually spend every waking hour looking to participate in the noble art of humping. Apparently, and with the exception of only two other species that I know of, *Homo Sapien* is the only mammal on planet earth that considers the sex act as some kind of recreational activity. I regret, however, that my clumsily simplistic action research was confined to mere earthly creatures, and so I cannot speak with such authority on the love-lives of our extra-terrestrial cousins, who for all I know, might be bonking away merrily from inter-galactic daybreak until dusk. Indeed, when you think about it, the facial expression on the friendly alien, *'ET'*, seemed to convey, to me at least, a rather distasteful picture of almost continual feverish masturbation. Anyway, I digress once more.

No, I'm afraid that when it comes to the process of canine procreation, the success or otherwise of 'blind dates' that have been arranged by optimistic would-be human breeders just isn't quite as simple as that. While it is certainly the case that most male dogs are generally 'up for it' at any stage, it really is the female who will determine if the act is to take place or not, which depends in turn on the specifics of her hormonal cycle and the resultant signals that she sends – or doesn't send – to her prospective suitor(s). In fact, the window of reproductive opportunity actually boils down to a mere two or three days during the bitch's 'season'.

So had we done our meticulous homework about Cindy's menstrual cycle or her ovulation dates? No, we most certainly had not. All we had done was noticed some stains on the carpet, looked up the local newspaper ad columns, and lifted fifty quid from the Royal Bank of Scotland.

Anyway, the absence of mathematical calculations and biological preparations apart, Cindy found herself pregnant, or 'up the skite' as my farm-reared mate Shug later put it somewhat less than diplomatically. Nan and I were delighted with the news, but Cindy couldn't have cared less. All she wanted was a good dinner, a decent walk and the occasional opportunity to hump either a visitor's leg or a thorn-free gorse bush.

However, she needed to know what was about to transpire approximately nine weeks from now. It was time for another chat.

In *Dogmanese*, of course.

Sharing Parenthood

'Life is tough enough without having someone kick you from the inside.'
(Rita Rudner, American Comedienne and Actress)

As most of us know, the human gestation period stretches to some nine months whereas, in the case of dogs, it lasts only about a quarter of that. If you are fortunate enough to have played your part in bringing children into this world, and blessed enough to have overseen the parallel process with your own dog, you will readily appreciate just how mind-blowingly joyous but incredibly different the contrasting processes happen to be.

It has to be said that, in comparison with the human reproductive process, dogs really don't hang about when it comes to delivering the goods. By way of illustration, less than a fortnight after the professional garden humping ceremony had taken place Robbie, our family vet, was able to tell us after a brief clinical examination that Cindy was well and truly pregnant. Seven weeks to go, he advised, so best get your obstetrics-related clobber together and rehearse your midwifery skills. I froze in terror. What had I done?

'But that's right in the middle of the British Open golf championship at Turnberry,' I spluttered incoherently in blind panic. 'And I'm supposed to be going with my mates on the Friday and Saturday!'

'Perhaps you should have thought about that when you got Cindy knocked up, then,' he replied without demonstrating the merest morsel of sympathy. 'It's called family planning, Ian.'

So here I was this time around in the local veterinary surgery, as opposed to the local doctors' surgery, having once again being given the joyful tidings of imminent parenthood. However, there was one slight difference, in that this time we would not be expecting either one male or one female human child but, in all probability, anything up to ten Labrador pups on account of Cindy herself having been born into a litter of such magnitude.

And so that was that. In less than a couple of months, we would have a scatter of manically loveable fluffy puppies running around all over the place. But what place? Where would we put them? And what did I know about delivering a succession of baby dogs, no doubt at some God-forsaken hour in the middle of the night while every vet in Scotland was fast asleep? My shock turned to terror, and my terror to panic. So I did what any sane man would do in such trying circumstances. I bought another book.

This particular publication was even more imaginatively-named than any of its utterly useless predecessors. *Caring For A Pregnant Dog* was the PR gem that its author had come up with, no doubt after many hours of cerebral contemplation and soul searching. The book attempted to teach me several things. It counselled me that the average canine gestation period was 63 days and advised me that I should treat Cindy 'normally' for the great bulk of that time, at least until the final two weeks. For example, I should continue to feed her normally, take her out for her constitutional walks, and try to keep her daily routine as normal as possible, for as long as possible. It also informed me that, as time went on, she would develop an expanding tummy and that I should refrain from encouraging her to chase toys or to participate in other such physically demanding exploits. I mean, how the devil would I have worked that out for myself, without having such a literary masterpiece lying on my bedside table?

Above all its constituent gems of wisdom, that wondrous publication taught me to do one thing in particular, and that was this. Without the merest shadow of a doubt, and no matter the prevailing circumstances, as soon as the big moment arrived I must go into an absolutely blind panic. No problem, I told myself, consider it done.

I gleaned that Cindy would become a bit leave-me-alone during the last couple of days of her pregnancy, that she would just want to curl up in some distant corner of the house, that she would start panting, spinning around in circles, drinking mega quantities of water and, perish the very thought and wash my mouth out with hot soapy water, that she would even go off her food. A Labrador Retriever going off its food? What?

And so with that last gem of highly dubious advice, another misguided publication found itself whirling through the air before diving into the kitchen bin with a thud.

'Ian, would you stop wasting money on books you never read?' opined my nearest-and-dearest. 'In six weeks' time, we'll have a horde of hungry pups to feed.'

'I think the collective noun you're looking for is 'litter', dear,' I retorted deeply hurt. 'You see, at least I've gone to the trouble of trying to find out how best to look after Cindy. Cindy and her HORDE! And without your assistance, it would seem. Let's see now, what precisely might you know about the subject matter, I wonder? Mmmmmmmm?'

'Quite a lot, actually,' Nan replied with one of the smug, supercilious smiles that she deploys whenever she feels a bit superior (which, quite understandably, is rather often).

'For example, the one I'm thinking about is presently drawing pictures with her crayons on the new dining room carpet, and pulling the heads off your precious roses so that she can give them to her granny. Now correct me if I'm wrong Ian, but aren't you supposed to be looking after your daughter at the moment? Yes that's right, the daughter to which I personally gave birth.'

'JILLIAN!' I bellowed. 'Stop it this instant!'

'Stop what, Daddy?' came the innocent reply.

'Just stop whatever it is you're doing, because your mum's getting annoyed with you.'

Nan just shook her head. 'And while you're at it, you might also want to think about getting control of your precious big dog, especially after what happened at the weekend.'

On that particular count, I really had no option but to concede that she had a valid point. Please allow me to explain. You see, on the previous Saturday, we had been invited to the wedding of a couple of our best friends, Tam and Lynn, and Nan had purchased a very expensive two-piece trouser suit for the occasion. Earlier that morning and in preparation for the necessarily laborious process of getting herself dressed, Nan had laid out her glorious new outfit on top of our king-sized duvet. Big mistake.

At some point between the girl from the local florist's shop delivering the carnations for our lapels, and Nan's emergence from the shower, she discovered to her horror that the now-knocked-up Cindy had decided to rearrange the new wedding clobber into a very ingeniously-conceived 'nest' in preparation for the arrival, some six weeks later, of her puppies. Wasn't that clever of her? Never before or since had I heard so many expletives being used so consecutively in so few sentences.

Anyway, back to the story. So, in recognition of my wife's very well made points regarding my dubious supervision and parenting capabilities, I decided that it was time to hand over custody of our fetchingly-mischievous daughter to the one who, as always, knew better.

I then put Cindy's lead over her head and popped her into the back of the car. It was time for us to have 'the conversation' and for Cindy to be the fortunate recipient of yet more of my pearls of acquired wisdom on the process of procreation. I wondered at the time if she actually realised just how fortunate she was to have such high quality counsel on tap.

'We're going for a big walk, lass,' I said to her, looking at her excited face in the rear view mirror.

'WOOF! WOOF!' Cindy replied in eager anticipation, her ears flapping and her big brown eyes bursting with ecstatic anticipation.

'And we're going to have a little talk about dogs having puppies!' I added.

When I looked in the mirror this time, I could see her ears

dropping like anvils and her eyes narrowing at the thought of the inevitable galloping tedium. She then let out the biggest sigh I had ever heard, and followed it up with an almighty yawn. I was deeply hurt.

'Okay, have it your way,' I said. 'We'll go for a walk first, but the deal is that we sit down and talk afterwards. Agree?'

'Okay, I suppose,' her unconvincing facial expression conceded, before adding another three unspoken words.

'If we must.'

I parked the car on a flattish grass banking in the country, about fifty metres away from the entrance to Cub's Glen, a well-known cavernous ravine on the River Lugar, famous for its excellent salmon fishing in the autumn months. Many a happy day and evening I spent 'up the Cub's', if often singularly unsuccessful from an angling point of view.

The glen itself only stretches for half a mile or so, from the top waterfall at Darmalloch farm, to the bottom stream beneath the 'Black Cliffs', where a ten-year-old schoolmate of mine died horrifically one summer's evening, falling from a tree on the cliff top whilst searching for crows' eggs, and landing prostrate on a huge rock in the middle of a big pool in the river some fifty metres below. I still shudder every time I walk past that spot.

Cindy and I followed the well-worn anglers' path which I had come to know in my adolescent years like the back of my hand. It really hadn't changed all that much, save for certain parts of the riverside path now being heavily overgrown and a few big trees now swaying proudly where puny saplings once clung to the banking for dear life. Parts of the riverbed had changed ever so slightly, no doubt as a consequence of the devastating floods of 1963, but these small details apart, it was just how I remembered it.

So here I was, many years later, together with my own wonderful big dog, and the glen still looked, felt and smelled almost exactly the same as it had done in the halcyon days of the early 'sixties. I wondered wistfully where all the years had gone.

As we meandered down through the glen, Cindy took the opportunity to dive into every single one of the dozen or so salmon pools which lay patiently in quiet anticipation of their seafaring charges returning to their assorted places of birth in September or, if the autumn rains came early and raised the water levels in spate, possibly as soon as mid-August. The whole place seemed very serene without the salmon leaping valiantly up the falls to the envious gasps of an army of exasperated anglers attempting to tempt them to take their bait.

About an hour later, we emerged from the foot of Cub's Glen into the open countryside beside the big walled orchard adjacent to an old farm, which Danny and I used to raid for scribe apples and Victoria plums in the endless summer days of our youth, but which now stood hopelessly overgrown and sadly bereft of forbidden fruit.

'This is where I used to come with my best mate Danny, when I was a wee boy,' I said dolefully to Cindy, automatically engaging our fledgling *Dogmanese*. She sat down on the grassy banking beside me and blinked, staring across the river towards the old orchard.

'And we never got caught once,' I added. 'Weren't we lucky?'

Cindy knew instinctively that the moment had come for our talk and, to her eternal credit, she had decided to listen attentively, or at least to give me the impression that she would try. She had walked for half an hour and swam for the other half, and she recognised that it was now time for her part of the bargain. And thus the serious lecture began.

'Cindy, you're pregnant,' I informed her. 'You are going to have a litter of pups in a few weeks' time.'

Her mouth opened ever-so-slightly, and she began panting gently. I could have sworn that she was giggling. Her eyes met mine.

'You don't say,' they teased me. 'The next thing you'll be telling me is that it was something to do with that big gorgeous dog in a strange garden, a couple of weeks ago!'

I drew her one of my serious looks. She smacked her lips in

partial acceptance of my facial scolding and drew in her tongue. Then she turned and looked at me in dutiful resignation. 'Okay, you've got ten minutes. Make it fascinating. Although even quite interesting will do.'

As we sat cheek-by-jowl on the lush banks of the River Lugar, Cindy became the fortunate recipient of the following riveting account of the canine maternity process.

'Okay Cindy, here goes', I began, attempting desperately to recall the most important snippets of information from the rejected doggy manual that would, by now, be resting alongside assorted worn-out carpets and defunct fridge-freezers in the local landfill site.

'I know everything just seems normal at the moment, Cindy,' I informed her, 'but trust me, it's all about to change. Your tummy will soon get bigger, and your body will undergo a lot of hormonal changes, which will make you a wee bit restless. And you'll probably want to clean yourself all the time. Mind you, you do that anyway, so nothing new there.'

I stared once more across the river towards the old orchard, and began reminiscing again, but immediately became conscious that Cindy was still staring at me.

'And?' her big eyes enquired, a bit impatiently.

'And, what? I asked. 'Oh yes, where was I?'

I was sure I noticed a very slight shake of the head, but I continued unflustered.

'And now, Cindy – this is the really weird part. You will lose your appetite.'

Cindy raised her eyebrows, in a kind of 'aye-that-will-be-right' expression, but I simply ploughed on regardless.

'I know, lass, it sounds strange to me too. In fact, it gets even more bizarre, because you might become a bit bad-tempered and even aggressive towards any strangers who come to the house.'

Cindy just continued to stare at me, her eyes attentive rather than fascinated, and her mouth slightly ajar. Her pupils weren't particularly dilated, probably around fifty-per-cent, signalling to me that she was listening politely, but with what I would call passing amusement rather than deep concentration. In fact, the only time she actually flinched was at the mention of the word 'strangers', at which point her pupils opened noticeably and she raised her eyebrows perceptibly.

I reassured her that I was not, in fact, referring specifically to the unfortunate little bin man, whom she hated anyway, and the arse of whose trousers she had once ripped off for reasons best known to herself. On the contrary, I informed her, I was referring to strangers in a much more general sense. She shrugged that one off with facial disdain and a heavy sigh. Again, I continued.

'When the big moment arrives – and, Cindy, do try to make it four in the afternoon rather than four in the bloody morning – your breathing will probably become a bit erratic, and you might find yourself closing your eyes, but I can assure you that you won't be sleeping.'

'And I can assure you that neither will you,' her big eyes replied with deep sincerity.

'Can I please continue?' I asked, rather irritated at this silent reciprocal aside.

'Thank you, Cindy,' I went on. 'When your contractions begin, the first birth might take a wee bit of time, but don't worry, because I'll be there to help you deliver your first wee puppy.'

'Well, that makes me feel a whole lot better,' she replied with a knowing, sanctimonious smile. 'After all, I just don't know how I would cope on my own.'

I wonder if she's being a bit sarcastic, I thought to myself. No matter, there's work to be done, Ian, so press on.

'Your contractions might vary a bit in intensity, but it is really important that you stay very calm, because if you don't and you get excited, your hormones will be all over the place, which will simply delay the next birth. Anyway, I'll be there with you to keep you nice and calm.'

Another raised eyebrow, another blink, another knowing

look. I'm sure she stifled another silly little giggle at that point, but I continued unperturbed.

'You will normally get a wee bit of rest between deliveries, although sometimes you'll find that two of your puppies will be born one immediately after the other, and so on.'

Semi-detached amusement, so I simply fired ahead.

'Now here's the scary bit. You might find that one or two of your pups don't breathe properly at first.'

Another raised eyebrow, a slightly more anxious look this time.

'But don't worry lass, because I'll be there to do one of two things, or maybe both. If this happens, I'll simply blow gently into their little mouths to put air down their windpipes and into their lungs, and that will help them to take their first breaths. And if that doesn't do the trick, I'll just dab a wee drop of brandy onto the tips of their tongues.'

'If you can spare any!' her big eyes said, but with more fun than sincerity.

At that point, and in light of her impressive patience over the last few minutes, it was Cindy's turn to reciprocate, by again engaging the non-verbal dimension of our very own secret language.

'Right, I've been really good and listened to all of this tosh,' she said. 'Now can we please get back into the car and go home for my dinner? I'm starving. And let's face it, for all I know I might have a dozen mouths to feed.'

I rolled my eyes skywards in quiet resignation, and fumbled in the pockets of my denims for the car keys. The obstetrics lesson was over, thankfully, for both of us.

Several weeks later and a few days short of the allotted date, I cleared out the cellar, created a wonderful little manger and furnished it lovingly with the obligatory fluffy blankets, clean toilet area, temporary heat lamp, and water and food dishes. Each night before I went to bed, I checked that all my clinical accoutrements were systematically laid out on the kitchen table, in eager anticipation of the big moment arriving at any time of day or night. A big plastic bowl, a bottle of detergent, another of disinfectant, a pair of rubber gloves, a dozen sterilised cloths, a wad of cotton wool and a litre bottle of Cognac brandy.

I came downstairs one morning, took *The Herald* out of the letter box, popped two slices of bread in the toaster and switched on the kettle. I opened the back door, went down the steps and turned the big key in the cellar door, where I was greeted by the magnificent sight of Cindy calmly breast-feeding her ten heavenly Labrador puppies. As they squeaked and squirmed contentedly beneath her, she gave a big wag of her tail.

Her bright eyes said it all. 'Who's a clever girl, then?'

Then her eyebrows dropped somewhat. 'And where were you, by the way?'

Tears welled up in my eyes as I approached her very gently. Her tail started thumping furiously on the cellar floor. Her posture was utterly relaxed and her demeanour was calmness personified. However, it was her eyes that radiated the sheer joy she was really feeling that wonderful morning.

'So isn't it about time you had that brandy, now?' they enquired.

Making Sense Of It All

'I never think of the future; it comes soon enough.'
(Albert Einstein, German Physicist and Humourist)

After my initial, if rather pleasant shock, I decided that I should immediately inspect the pups one by one, to check if they were all alive and well. I had read up on what to look for, beginning with the rather clinical task of counting ears, limbs and other such like appendages then moving on to the more vital pointers such as heartbeats and breathing patterns. That was when, to my great sadness, I discovered that two of Cindy's pups had been stillborn.

I had been advised by Robbie that this might well happen, and that it was simply nature's way of regulating the size of the litter to align itself with the mother's maternal care capacity. I wondered at the time if the poor little things would have made it, if only I had been present to assist Cindy in the childbirth process, and/or to administer discreet quantities of self-propelled oxygen and French brandy. I would never know though, would I?

I suppose I did get the answer I was looking for later that very same day, after my umpteenth visit to our canine manger-in-the-cellar, when I discovered to my horror that another two pups had perished, this time unwittingly suffocated underneath the body weight of their mother. As I removed the two unfortunate babies from below Cindy's undercarriage, she simply sniffed at them, licked them goodbye and rather clinically returned to the pragmatics of feeding the six remaining survivors.

I immediately phoned Robbie, whose chosen few words were

a masterpiece of blunt pragmatism, but which succeeded superbly in putting the whole thing into stark perspective.

'Ian, you have just witnessed an incredible natural phenomenon in two distinct phases, the wonders of childbirth and the brutal but necessary reality of natural selection. This is simply mother nature's way of ensuring that Cindy can cope as a mother, and that the surviving pups will thrive.'

I thanked him for his candour, and sought reassurance that the rest of the litter would be okay.

'Cindy now has six healthy puppies that she can cope with, and they will make six families very, very happy,' said Robbie. 'Now, if you'll excuse me, Kathy has just put my soup in a bowl and if there's one thing I hate, it's cold soup. Bye.' A click on the phone line and he was off to sup his Scotch broth.

One rainy evening a few weeks later, as my two children and Cindy's six were chasing each other manically all around our dining room with Nan and her friend Alison allegedly in charge of the chaotic proceedings, I sat in my favourite armchair in the lounge, sipping a malt whisky, with the hopelessly devoted Cindy welded to my side. I was lost in deep thought and she was just mightily relieved to get some well-deserved peace and quiet. She snuggled up at my feet and instantly broke my trance. I patted her magnificent forehead and she turned towards me. I gazed deep into her big brown eyes.

'What are you thinking, Cindy?' I said.

'Only another week to go, and then you can put them on real food,' she replied through her eyes as usual. 'My nipples are killing me.'

'You'll be fine, lass!' I said reassuringly. 'By this time next week, they'll be munching on solid puppy food and you'll be back in the house with us.'

Her tail gave a 'thump-thump-thump,' on the floor, as she looked up at me. Cindy was happy, and I knew it. But how did I actually know that, I asked myself quizzically, yet again? I just did, that's how.

'I know you're happy with life, Cindy, and that's all that

matters. End of story,' I said aloud. 'And I will always know how you're feeling. And you will always know how I'm feeling, won't you lass? Because we speak to each other in our secret language. We speak *Dogmanese*, and not a single, solitary soul out there knows a thing about it, except us!'

Another 'thump-thump-thump,' of the tail, another few gentle pants, another heart-warming 'smile' of contentment.

At that point, a much darker thought hit home, one that had tried on numerous occasions to waft its pernicious way into my highly imaginative cerebrum, but to which my often wavering powers of positive thought had contrived thus far to deny access. However, for some strange reason on this occasion, I decided to let it in and see what it had to say for itself.

The horrific thought was this. It's great to have my own big dog now, and for both of us to have our own secret language. However some day, hopefully many, many years down the line, one of us is going to pop our clogs and then we simply won't have each other anymore.

'What happens then, Cindy?' I asked her very tentatively. 'How am I going to cope without my big dog to talk to?' Cindy's eyes seemed to recess slowly into their sockets. She smacked her lips, stretched gently and stood up by my side.

'In fact, it could be me that kops it before you,' I continued. 'What would happen then to our secret language?' Her eyes narrowed further. She raised one paw just perceptibly above the carpet and started panting rapidly. Cindy was becoming anxious and agitated.

'Sorry, lass, I'm just upsetting you,' I said.

'Yes you are, and I don't like it when you talk like that,' her eyes replied.

Then they told me something else entirely, something I really hadn't expected.

'Perhaps you should make sense of it all. You know, so that Nan and Jillian and others can understand it some day,' she suggested.

'What do you mean, Cindy?' I asked, somewhat perplexed.

'Why don't you do what you humans always like to do?' she asked.

'And what's that, Cindy?' I enquired, totally intrigued.

'Write it down on pieces of paper,' she said. And then she added, 'Just in case.'

Classical Dogmanese & How It Works

'Get your facts first, then you can distort them as you please.'
(Mark Twain, American Author and Humourist)

'Do you know something, Cindy?' I asked her rhetorically, 'I really don't know where you get all these weird ideas from. But I do have to hand it to you, this latest one is a thing of beauty. I will indeed do as you say, and write it all down on paper. We'll call it *'Classical Dogmanese'*. Sheer genius!'

Cindy stood up, stretched her athletic frame to maximum extension and lifted her head confidently, simultaneously raising one eyebrow and dilating her nostrils. She radiated her superior gaze directly towards me.

'Yes, I suppose I am a bit of a genius, now that I come to think about it. Is there a dog chew in the cupboard there, by any chance?' she enquired, by merely casting a knowing glance in that particular direction. 'It's surely the least a genius can expect before she retires for the night to feed six hungry mouths.'

As she gorged on the meaty chew, she looked up at me, smacked her lips and added, 'Oh yes, and a little evening stroll wouldn't go amiss either.'

As I slipped the leash over her neck, I laughed, 'You, madam, have got the whole thing sussed, haven't you?' Her tail wagged excitedly, as she waited for me to open the back door.

So there it was then, the big master plan. We had already invented our own new and very secret language. All I had to do now was commit it to paper. It would be a piece of cake. Wouldn't it?

The thing was that I had not so much 'invented' *Dogmanese*, but built the whole thing up through a few years' experiential learning based on speculative observation of canine body language. And of course, all of this borne out of the utmost psychological necessity by the perplexed beholder, and driven by an amazing emotional bond between one mere mortal of the *Homo Sapien* persuasion and another of *Canis Familiaris*. Man's best friend confides in dogs' best friend, if you like.

I did realise, of course, that *Dogmanese* had not developed, thus far at least, to an academic level that would attract unmanageable numbers of aspiring university students to crave for a Ph.D. in the bloody thing, but at least it was a start. I also realised something else entirely, something that I didn't particularly like admitting to myself, and that was the fact that the verbal/non-verbal hybrid lingo onto which Cindy and I had stumbled, undoubtedly had a very finite shelf life, the precariously brief duration of which would inevitably be determined by which one of us found ourselves pushing up the daisies first.

In other words, when the grim reaper decided to call upon one of us, *Dogmanese* would simply disappear into the gloomy forest mists along with his preferred first victim, as an unavoidable consequence of the magical bond between Cindy and me being ripped asunder. Therefore, without a question of a doubt, she was correct. I had to do what humans do, and 'write it down on pieces of paper', otherwise it would be lost for ever, which would be a complete tragedy. What a clever dog, I informed her, and she readily agreed with my astute assessment.

And so, with the human race still eagerly awaiting the global onslaught of laptop computers, *Microsoft Word* and digital technology, I marched into the John Menzies' bookstore in Ayr's High Street and purchased a big fancy notebook. It cost me a bloody fortune, one-pound-seventy-five-pence as I recall, which would have got me about four pints of beer in those days. As I strode purposefully out of the stationery shop, my size nines suddenly screeched to a halt. For some strange reason, they made me retrace my steps, and I marched up to the counter, where I parted with another three-quid for a Parker pen, and then marched back out again. If I was going to translate *Dogmanese* into the Queen's English, it was about to get the full treatment.

I pondered long and hard before I commenced the translation process. I had more false starts than an Olympic sprinter on forbidden steroids. Excitement soon turned to frustration, then frustration to exasperation. I lost count of the number of curled-up, scribbled sheets of paper that found themselves hurtling through the air in the general direction of the dustbin, and with increasing velocity and venom as the days went on. I was getting nowhere.

Then one evening after dinner, the penny dropped.

'You're trying too hard, Ian,' I said aloud to myself. 'You're treating this exercise as if *Dogmanese* is actually a word-based language, rather than recognising what it really is. It is purely a means of communicating between a man and a dog, one that relies principally on a mix of human observation of canine body language, and vice versa, and some verbal utterances thrown in for good measure.'

I nodded at Cindy in smug satisfaction who, in turn, tilted her head from one side to the other in quizzical fashion, then raised both eyebrows sharply as the penny landed with a metallic 'clunk'.

'Cindy, I'm going to start by simply writing down all of the things I've seen and learned from your body language. I'm going to think very hard about these things, about your posture, and your head, and your face, and your mouth, and your bark, and your tail, and your ears. And I'm going to try to write down what I think each signal you send me actually means, which will be quite difficult to do because it's all about how these signals interact with each other. And I'm going to concentrate particularly closely on your eyes, because it's your eyes that you use more than anything else to tell me things. Isn't it, lass?'

Cindy smiled at me. 'Might be,' she teased.

So I gathered together all the research findings and various notes I had scribbled down over the past few years, pushed the nib of my new Parker pen into position and opened my big fancy notebook.

'Here we go, then,' I announced to Cindy, and set about chronicling everything I had ever learned about how my own dog had contrived to communicate with me, and me with her.

The plan was a simple one. Once I had catalogued all the relevant information about body language and associated communicative signals, I would then try to build up a sort of '*Dogmanese* Glossary' of all the verbal and, in particular, the non-verbal signals that I had come to recognise, see what it looked like and just take it from there.

I decided to start with the very basic observations that really didn't need a great deal of thought or interpretation. Purely by way of example, an intoxicated amoeba wearing deep-filter sunglasses would be able to observe and conclude that when a dog crouches with its head downwards, mouth open and tongue extended, and its backside raised upwards with its tail wagging feverishly, it wants to play. On the other hand, if you meet a strange Rottweiler in a padlocked builders' yard and it greets you with its hackles raised, tail rigid and trembling, and lips curled to reveal its gums, and a set of salivating gnashers that could rip an ancient oak tree from a country courtyard, then it probably doesn't want to play. At least not in a way that you and I would find particularly recreational.

So sticking with the basics, and leaving the more academic stuff to the animal behavioural buffs, I just started scribbling. Before long, and to my great delight, my Parker pen was soon in overdrive and in need of a refill, as was my empty glass.

The following are only a few illustrations of some of the messages I had picked up over the years from Cindy, and how I had interpreted these. No more and no less.

What Cindy's Face Told Me
- When her mouth was opened slightly, the tip of her pink tongue just showing, and she was breathing very gently, she was happy, relaxed and at peace with the world.

- When her mouth was closed, and she was again breathing gently, but this time with her head stalk-still, she was in a highly alert state and taking a very keen interest in the proceedings.
- On the very odd occasion when her lips were curled, she was most displeased at someone or something, invariably a third party stranger or an unusual noise.
- When she was licking my face, she was doing one of two quite different things. Firstly, she might have been telling me that I was the bee's knees, the big hero, the 'special' one. Secondly, and much less favourably for my ego, she might simply have been wanting her dinner.
- When she was yawning regularly and repeatedly, she was either deeply bored with the proceedings, or perhaps even a little bit anxious about something (such as a thunder and lightning storm, for example).

What Cindy's Ears Told Me
- When her ears were pinned back, she was really quite unhappy or worried about something, and I always sensed that she was on some kind of 'standby'.
- When her ears were alert and thrust slightly forward, she was in a highly attentive state, taking stock of recent events and just waiting with bated breath to see what was about to happen next.
- When her ears went up and down repeatedly, she was again sizing up the situation, but possibly a bit more anxiously this time.

What Cindy's Body Language Told Me
- If her hackles were raised from the top of her head to the tip of her tail, she was telling the object of her attention that she was getting seriously pissed off, and that if the annoying behaviour didn't stop, she was quite prepared to demonstrate just how serious she was.
- If her gait was as rigid as a poker, and her head was held high,

she was at her cocky, confident, superior best and wanted everyone to know just how very fortunate they were to be in her glorious company.

- When she rolled over on her back, legs apart and her tail wagging furiously, she was being totally submissive, and happily acknowledging the higher position she had afforded me in the pecking order.
- If she crouched down in front of me, with her head and front paws on the carpet, her backside up in the air, and her tail swishing frenetically, that was the quite unmistakeable play look.

What Cindy's Tail Told Me

- If her tail was sloping slightly downwards and wagging gently from side to side, she was happy, contended and relaxed.
- If her tail was sticking straight out rigidly, but with the slightest quiver (her 'rattlesnake' tail, as Nan and I used to call it), she was a bit unsure and untrusting of someone or something, and trying to signal assertiveness.
- If her tail was hanging straight down and only wagging a wee bit pathetically, she was either feeling slightly under the weather, or a bit down in the dumps about something.
- On the very odd occasion when her tail was curled right between her hind legs (or 'welded', as we would say), she was really quite frightened about something and looking for my reassurance, or perhaps even my physical intervention, in a potentially threatening situation.
- When her tail started wagging so energetically that her big backside actually followed it from side to side, she was really in her element, and signalling that she was absolutely over the moon just to be with me.

What Cindy's Eyes Told Me

- When she was staring directly at me (or at someone else), she was radiating confidence to the point of smugness, or even assertiveness at times.

- When she was quite deliberately looking away from me (or particularly from another dog), trying everything possible to avoid all eye contact, she was in her submissive pose, or perhaps even frightened.
- If her eyelids were blinking fairly rhythmically, she was simply sizing up the situation and considering all her options.
- When her pupils were contracting, she was either becoming bored and disinterested with my conversation (for example, if I was rabbiting on about a football match), or signalling her displeasure at my latest hare-brained idea.
- When her pupils were dilating, she was signalling keen interest, enthusiasm and even excitement.
- When her pupils suddenly opened all the way to maximum aperture, or her 'full-beam' mode as I used to call it, they were actually <u>screaming</u> some very, very important message to me. The full-beam look would come on in an instant and without any warning, I think for optimum effect, and would often give me a nasty jolt.
- When her pupils went into a rapidly oscillating pattern of dilations and contractions, she was 'speaking' to me with her eyes, and that was when I would receive a whole host of messages from her. The experience was utterly hypnotic, and it would be impossible for me to explain it in words, since I am convinced that there was also a 'sixth sense' dimension at play.

Now, when you see all this stuff written down on 'pieces of paper', it looks fairly straightforward, doesn't it? Well you can forget that notion for a start. And for four principal reasons:

First Reason: I have listed only 24 examples of the numerous body signals and messages that I received from Cindy over the years, and which I came to learn and recognise.

Second Reason: All of the above is about one communication dimension only, namely the physical signals that Cindy somehow managed to send in my direction.

Third Reason: In my own experience anyway, very few of the above and other signals actually mean all that much on their own. For example, I could only really tell for sure if Cindy was feeling anxious or frightened about something, _if_ her tail was curled beneath her hind legs, _and_ her ears were pinned back, _and_ she was panting, _and_ she was yawning, _and_ she was whimpering, _and_ she was trying everything possible to avoid eye contact with the object of her anxiety.

Fourth Reason: Finally, and most importantly of all, I found that the real magic of meaningful communication between Cindy and me lay in the incredibly complex matrix of interaction between our respective postures, voices, ears - and particularly, both sets of eyes.

However hopelessly deprived I happen to be of any academic training whatsoever in the incredibly complex field of animal psychology, there is one thing about which I am absolutely certain from my own experience, and it is this. To really understand the wonders of communication between human beings and dogs, it is no use thinking of two separate message-sending/message-receiving processes, namely, _man-to-dog_ and _dog-to-man_.

The remarkably fluent 'visual conversations' that Cindy and I somehow learned to conduct were most certainly a whole lot more complex than one of us providing a wee snippet of information, and the other reciprocating with another such gem. Instead, I am convinced that our actual conversations were the product of one single organic process into which two willing communicators fed by offering and receiving various pieces of recognisable and meaningful information, on a dynamic and continuous basis, and then sustaining a two-way flow of such information through a very complex matrix of verbal and non-verbal signals.

While I am very reluctant to try to over-simplify our 'visual conversations', I will concede that they did seem to follow a fairly standard pattern, normally along the following lines.

One of us, normally myself, would start the process by conveying a piece of information, most often verbally, but sometimes through my own body energy which in turn seemed to be a function of my 'mood' at the time

Cindy would recognise my verbal words and/or my non-verbal signals, or at least some of them, then interpret what I was rambling (or gesticulating) on about.

She would then answer me, through a range of 'soft' signals emanating from her superbly diverse body language that I had taken the time to study and recognise, the clearest of which came particularly from her eyes.

I would continue the conversation, again normally in mere human words, and she would respond as before, the two of us often (but admittedly not always) then being able somehow to develop and sustain a flow of meaningful verbal/visual exchanges.

On some occasions, normally when my emotions had been running high, as was often the case in those difficult times, it would be Cindy herself who would terminate the conversation by suddenly dilating her pupils to full aperture, which in turn would SCREAM an important message to me, normally in the form of some kind of 'wake-up call'.

So there you have it, an extremely convoluted process, and all rather recklessly distilled down into a few human words for your own delectation. However, I do have to be completely honest here and admit that, even after several years of trying, I still fell somewhat short of being able to make complete sense of it all, at least in a way that would lend itself to being recorded unfailingly error-free in my John Menzies' notebook.

And so I was left with no option but to concede that there was probably something else going on here as well, something that my own simple human brain was nowhere near sophisticated enough to comprehend. However successful or otherwise I had become in connecting dynamic communicative signals between Cindy and me with some sort of pattern of cognitive progression, there was also a 'sixth sense' dimension at play.

To illustrate this very point, allow me if you will to rehearse one such 'conversation' that took place between Cindy and me, and which I remember to this day with particular clarity, because it was one that resulted in me receiving a very powerful message from a four-year-old dog. Indeed, it turned out to be such an important conversation that it would actually revolutionise my young wife's life.

'Cindy!' *Alert eyes. Ears forward. Standing to attention. Tail straight out but relaxed. Mouth very slightly ajar. Breathing gently. Pupils at fifty per cent.*

'Cindy, sit.' *Sits down. Mouth closes. Eyes still alert. Gentle breathing continues. Pupils narrow very slightly.*

'Cindy, can I ask you a question?' *A very slight tilt of the head. Pupils widen very slightly.*

'Do you think Nan is a bit happier now?' *Staring straight at me. Pupils narrow again. She blinks a total of four times, and yawns twice. Cindy is not sure, possibly realises the importance of the question, and begins to feel a little bit anxious at the thought.*

'What's wrong, lass?' *Her ears go back slightly. Her mouth opens and she starts panting gently. I stroke her head. She licks my arm.*

'Do I need to do something else to help her?' *Panting stops immediately. Mouth closes, nostrils widen. Pupils dilate noticeably. Head tilts, first to one side then the other.*

'I do, don't I?' *Stares at me intensely, gaze unwavering. I look at her eyes. Her pupils contract then dilate, contract again then dilate again, over and over and over. I am mesmerised.*

'Cindy, I'm worried that she'll really hurt herself because of the way she walks. The doctor says that she's really going to damage her hips and even her spine if she continues to shuffle and haul her legs around.' *Cindy continues staring at me. Listens attentively. Motionless.*

'But you'll remember that one night last week I mentioned getting a wheelchair, and she burst into tears and called me an insensitive bastard. I just don't know what to do now, Cindy, I really don't.' *Cindy stares at me. Mouth closed. Pupils narrower than before. Body completely motionless, except for the steady rise and fall of her diaphragm. Then her pupils dilate. They suddenly become enormous, like car headlights in full beam.*

'YES YOU DO!' *she shouts, without moving her lips.*

I jump, slightly startled.

'Okay, I'll speak to her again tonight.' *Mouth opens. Pink tongue appears. Pupils still dilated. Cindy is smiling at me. She is pleased with me. It took a while, she smirks, but we eventually got there.*

I put Jillian to bed at about eight o'clock that evening, then poured Nan and myself a glass of wine. Cindy sat on the floor between us, facing me rather than Nan.

'No time like the present,' she said with her eyes. 'Do it now!'

By bedtime, and after more than a few tears, I had managed to persuade Nan that getting a wheelchair might not be such a bad thing after all, and might actually enhance certain aspects of her quality of life and independence. We eventually agreed that she would contact her Occupational Therapist the very next day.

I let Cindy out into the back garden for a few minutes, to do her 'business', then commanded her to go to bed. She marched into it without hesitation.

'Thanks for the advice pal, but always remember who's the boss around here, won't you?' I said to her authoritatively.

Cindy curled up in her fluffy blanket with her head resting on both front paws. Her tail wagged ever-so-gently. However, it was her eyes that said it all, as they always seemed to do. 'Who's a clever girl, then?'

I climbed into bed, kissed Nan goodnight, turned away from her and lay there holding back the tears for what seemed like an eternity. I had just persuaded my young wife to do the very last thing on earth that I would ever have wished for her. To spend the rest of her life confined to a wheelchair.

And that, folks, was *Dogmanese* in action.

Restoring The Gender Balance

'A boy is a magical creature – you can lock him out of your workshop,
but you can't lock him out of your heart.'
(Allan Beck, American Author)

Cindy was right, of course. You never can tell what's waiting around the next corner, as Nan and I were about to discover only a few weeks later. So, before continuing with my mission to 'write things down on pieces of paper', there was one other little matter that required my more immediate attention.

You see, one of my biggest fears about Multiple Sclerosis – and, trust me, I had a few – was its possible effect on Nan's condition should she ever become pregnant again. Those fears were, of course, very well-founded since it had been either shortly before or after becoming pregnant that she had actually contracted MS. And, into the bargain, I still retained vivid memories of my poor late aunt, who had also developed MS at or around the time of her second pregnancy, and who had passed away only a tragically short time afterwards.

Therefore, some three-and-a-bit years after our little blonde princess had entered this world, Nan and I had taken stock of all the advice we had received – both solicited and completely unsolicited – on the subject matter.

On the one hand, the various merchants of well-intentioned but hideously misplaced doom were counselling us not to be so bloody stupid, and simply to content ourselves with what we already had, which was of course a wonderful little family of two adult human beings and one delightful child of the same species, together with one behaviourally-stretched but ultra-loyal canine minder-cum-amateur psychoanalyst sitting protectively beside our cosy fireplace.

On the other hand, though, was the small matter of Nan's (and my own, if I'm being really honest) burning desire to provide Jillian with a wee brother or sister. Sure, there was a risk that a further pregnancy might adversely affect Nan's already precarious neurological condition, but that was by no means certain, and into the bargain, just what effect might such an abstention have on her frail but steadily-improving psychological outlook and self-esteem?

A very considered letter from one of Nan's umpteen medical advisers, in response to one from myself to himself, attempted to put the whole thing into perspective. *'I would not assess the risk of further neurological damage through pregnancy as very high, but it is significant. Alternatively, should Mrs McMurdo be deprived of her obvious wish to have a second child, there is always the risk that she may be left with a psychological vacuum. The decision, therefore, is not any easy one for Mrs McMurdo and you to make, but it is properly one that you must make yourselves.'*

I simply lost count of the number of discussions Nan and I had about whether or not we ought to try for another child. Spontaneous, romantic love-making, this was not. Our entire physical relationship at that time simply revolved around one quaint little question. Should I get Nan knocked up again?

The thing was, though, that I was the only one asking that particular question, since Nan was absolutely unwavering in her firm response, every time the question popped up. Yes I should, end of story, so let's go upstairs and leave the condoms in the sock drawer. It really was a great offer, when you think about it, but alas, it wasn't quite as simple as that.

So I did what any intelligent, academically-trained, pragmatic scientist would do in the circumstances. I asked my dog.

It was a Saturday morning and, quite deliberately, I had decided that today's hike-in-the-woods would be taking place at the self-same location as that which witnessed our hypnotic trance in the car all that time ago, namely, Dalblair Bridge. However, rather than sit blubbering at the wheel as happened on that awful previous occasion, this time I marched Cindy away up into the hills and well beyond any semblance of civilisation as we know it, save for a few idiotic hares scurrying hither and thither in no particular direction, but at quite enormous speeds. What stupid things they are, hares, but I digress once again.

After about two hours of brisk walking, or 7.2 miles to be precise (my ambient dog-walking rate is about 3.6 miles per hour, you see – what a complete anorak I have become these days), I deposited my weary backside on a prostrate fence post. Without needing any invitation, Cindy, who would undoubtedly have walked at least twice as far as I had by that time, slumped down beside me for a breather.

'Cindy,' I said to her quietly, 'I need a wee bit of advice.'

'Here we bloody go again,' her big honest face appeared to say. 'I should charge a hundred quid an hour for this, I really should. Okay, what is it this time?'

'Nan wants another baby,' I informed her. Cindy's eyes lit up immediately, and her bottom jaw dropped noticeably. Bloody hell, not another one, her face commented involuntarily, but revealingly.

'You might remember, Cindy, that Nan became ill around the time she was pregnant with Jillian, and I'm afraid that she might become ill again if we have another baby,' I said to her with a heavy sigh.

'So what is it that you're telling me here, exactly?' her big eyes quizzed me, with what appeared to be a genuinely puzzled expression. 'Are you saying that you know for sure that her illness was caused by her pregnancy?'

'No, I'm not saying that at all, because I really don't know for sure,' I said in response to her very astute and searching question. 'All I know is that her illness and her pregnancy both occurred around the same time, that's all.'

'Okay,' my canine counsellor continued, 'then are you saying that you wish Nan had never had Jillian in the first place?'

'No, of course I'm not!' I retorted in pure indignation. 'I love

Jillian to bits. And you do too. I simply can't imagine life without her now. That's an awful thing to say, Cindy.'

'Just asking,' she teased silently, turning her head away from me a moment too late to conceal a naughty little snigger.

'So what do you think then, smart arse?' I continued. 'Should we have another baby, or not? Come on, answer the bloody question.'

'Your decision, big man,' she replied.

'I know it is, Cindy,' I snapped. 'I know it's my decision. What I'm asking you is what that decision should be. If it's not too much trouble, that is. Because you see, Cindy, I just don't know what to do. And that's why I'm asking you. Get the picture?'

At that moment, Cindy stood up straight, stretched herself, and turned to face me head-on. Her tail went rigid, she raised her head and opened her mouth. Then, in an instant, her pupils dilated to full aperture.

'YES YOU DO!' her eyes screamed at me.

I literally jumped. 'For God's sake, Cindy, don't do that! I nearly piss myself every time you do that …….. that thing …… with your eyes.'

'Well, you did ask me, didn't you?'

'Yes I did, Cindy. So, what's your answer, then?'

'You know the answer. It's staring you in the face.'

So I enquired sheepishly, 'So we should go for it, then?'

'Of course you should!' she laughed. 'Isn't it about time the gender balance was restored in the McMurdo household? If I was in your position, I would be going mad with all these hormonal women around me all day.'

'But how do you know it will be a wee boy?' I asked her even more tentatively.

Cindy simply grinned one of her big supercilious grins. 'Right, enough of this crap. Let's make our way back to the car. It's nearly dinner time, and my stomach thinks its throat has been cut.'

I stretched and stood up, completely bewildered yet again by a wordless conversation, but one that would ultimately prove to be life-changing for my whole family, and life-forming for our wonderful son who would grace this world almost one year later. Cindy was fast becoming my principal source of inspiration.

And *Dogmanese* had already become its vehicle.

Cutting To The Chase

*'Therefore, since brevity is the soul of wit, and tediousness the limbs
and outward flourishes, I will be brief.'*
(William Shakespeare, Hamlet)

Now, for those of you who have got this far through my quaint little tale, I am assuming that you have come to one of the only two possible conclusions about my alleged 'conversations' with the ten-quid puppy.

<u>Conclusion 1:</u> For some strange reason which, admittedly, I have only been able to explain rather clumsily in any sensible way at all, those conversations between Cindy and me really did take place, and actually did guide me in a purely practical as well as a deeply emotional sense.

<u>Conclusion 2:</u> My Dolittlesque ramblings are so utterly ridiculous and far-fetched that you simply want to tell your friends that you actually managed to read this tosh, before they discover that its hopelessly insane author was eventually clad in a straightjacket and frogmarched away to some high-security sanatorium in the wilderness of Caithness.

It's your choice, buddy. However, do allow me to clarify my intentions (and non-intentions) before we delve any further into the evolution of the fascinating little language that is *Dogmanese*.

To begin with, it is certainly not my lifelong ambition to convert the *Dogmanese* 'agnostics' out there. Rather, it is simply my sworn mission to record my own bewildering experiences of the incredible bond that, somehow, I managed to develop with Cindy. So, for those of you who are fully paid-up members of the Conclusion (2) club, I wish you many happy hours of reading this little piece of pure unadulterated fiction.

Alternatively, for those in the Conclusion (1) corner, you will clearly have recognised what I am talking about, and just how important my communication with Cindy had become by that stage. However, you will also have clocked the tragic inevitability that lay somewhere down this newly-constructed road which, some sad day soon, would surely run out of tarmac.

In attempting to write this book, there was one major challenge I needed to grapple with from the very outset. That was, of course, just how I was going to tackle the potentially very tricky matter of setting down, in words and sentences and paragraphs and chapters, the essential features of what is, in large measure at least, a non-verbal communication medium. In an earlier chapter, I tried to give you a flavour, not only of the NVC messages that passed between Cindy and me during our increasingly profound 'discussions', but also how these translated into the VC language that we mere humans tend to use to rationalise everything that moves, and indeed some that don't.

I think you'll agree that for me to continue to deploy this exceedingly convoluted methodology of chronicling every single detail of Cindy's body language signals, and then spuriously to transmogrify each and every one of these into the Queen's English, would constitute an unnecessarily cumbersome and laborious process. Worse still, your next of kin might well find you hanging by the neck-tie from the kitchen rafters, as a sad consequence of your valiant attempts to make sense of this whole communicative labyrinth.

Therefore, and given that by this stage you will either have bought my half-baked explanation of my connection with Cindy or you will not, what I intend to do from hereon in is simply to paraphrase the actual 'conversations' themselves, trusting you to trust me that they actually took place for real.

The alternative is not one you would wish to contemplate, involving as it would the construction of a tome of *War and Peace* proportions, and the reader's inevitable and spiralling descent into a world of confusion, paranoia and galloping insanity.

So, with your permission, I simply intend to cut to the chase from this juncture onwards, and regale you with a few memorable tales of Cindy's derring-do and, of course, the very conversations that accompanied them. Is that okay with you?

Excellent. Then I'll begin.

That Sinking Feeling

'Drown not thyself to save a drowning man.'
(Ancient Proverb)

As I opened the back door of our not-quite-but-nearly-new yellow Ford Capri, Cindy didn't need much coaxing to jump onto the tartan travelling rug that lay strewn across the rear seat. Poor Max did, though. As he looked at me with his big sad eyes, I grabbed him by the buttocks and shoved him in beside his new best pal.

'I want my mummy and daddy,' his big sad eyes seemed to say.

Max was a huge, sturdy, black Labrador dog, who had been temporarily deposited on our proverbial doorstep by our good friends Andy and Susan, as the two lovebirds sped off on a jet plane for a dirty weekend in downtown Amsterdam.

Max really was a magnificent canine specimen, having spent the bulk of his three-and-a-half years retrieving newly-deceased pheasants from the fatal consequences of the deadly projectiles that regularly exploded from Andy's double-barrelled shotgun. Max was a serious gun dog, and a mighty handsome one into the bargain.

That day, however, he was an emotional wreck, having spent the whole of his very first night trembling nervously indoors instead of chilling out as usual in his custom-built wooden kennel, and also having deposited on our kitchen floor the most enormous canine shit the world has ever seen. When I stumbled my eye-rubbing way through to the kitchen at seven-fifteen the next morning, Cindy was lying in the far corner with a plastic clothes peg over her nose.

'For any favour, clean it up and throw that basket-case outside,' she said, rather more nasally than usual.

'I'm sure he'll be fine once you take him a big walk,' was Nan's solitary contribution, after she had wheeled herself through some thirty minutes later, and immediately before burying her head in *The Herald* and her teeth in a toast-and-banana sandwich.

'Aye, right,' I replied in my superbly well-developed dismissive style, which used to drive her mad and still does to this day, I'm delighted to say.

So there the three of us were, the pack leader at the steering wheel, my yellow-haired second-in-command perched confidently in the back seat behind me, and our newly acquired, stressed-out companion twitching-and-shivering beside her, and beside himself in anxiety.

'Right, doggies, where will we go this morning?' I enquired rhetorically, but with added enthusiasm in a valiant attempt to snap the teeth-chattering Max out of his galloping insecurity.

'How about a big walk along the River Ayr?' I enquired, looking at both sets of eyes in my rear view mirror.

'WOOF! WOOF!' barked Cindy excitedly, exhibiting a pair of dilated pupils and another of alert ears.

'Whimper, whimper,' whined Max through his trembling incisors, a message clearly replicated in his big worried eyes.

'God save us,' I muttered silently, 'this is going to be a fun ride.'

As I looked in the mirror once more, Cindy just winked at me. 'He'll be fine, big man. Just leave it to me. *Cindy Power* is about to explode into action again!'

'You'd better behave yourself today, madam,' I giggled.

Some twenty minutes later, we were parked a hundred metres or so from the Stair Inn, a wonderfully quaint Ayrshire hostelry that served excellent food for discerning diners, and a selection of tasty ales for thirsty walkers, and still does to this very day, I am pleased to say. As I opened the back door of the Capri, Cindy bolted out expectantly, but Max just sat there like as if he had lost his wallet.

'Come on, big fella,' I said, and eventually coaxed him out of the car.

And it was at that point that the most amazing thing happened. He raised his snout skywards, sniff-sniff-sniffed the clean autumnal air and turned to look at me. Within seconds, his whole body language changed completely. His gait suddenly became erect and confident, his bushy black tail began swishing at forty-five degrees, and at forty-five miles per hour into the bargain, and his eyes lit up like searchlights at half-two on a winter's morning. Max was in his comfort zone again, the great outdoors.

As I stood staring in intrigued admiration at the spectacular transformation, he suddenly turned on his heels and bolted.

Offski.

Cindy and I just stood there open-mouthed in amazement, and within a few seconds all we could see was Max's enormous backside disappearing into the five-foot-high ferns that sheltered the riverbank.

'He's really quite biddable,' were the last words that Susan had uttered before jumping into the car with Andy, *en route* to Glasgow Airport.

Well, we're certainly about to find out, I thought to myself. Perhaps I should have put his leash on, I reflected momentarily before deciding on my next strategy, which was to fly into a blind panic. A good ten minutes later, and he was still nowhere to be seen. Holy shit, I thought to myself, what have I done?

'What am I going to tell Andy and Susan, if he has just pissed off and doesn't come back?' I blurted somewhat incoherently to Cindy.

'I told you, just leave it to me,' she replied reassuringly, and stormed off in hot pursuit of her new playmate.

'Oh brilliant!' I said aloud. 'Absolutely bloody brilliant, Ian! Now you've lost the two of them. Give yourself a bag of sweeties, you complete prick!'

As my anxiety levels steadily escalated and my imagination began to run increasingly amok, it would be impossible to begin to explain my relief when I then saw both of them emerging from the ferns and climbing up the steep incline of the riverbank, tails wagging away merrily.

'CINDY! MAX!' I shouted. 'COME HERE!'

Both bolted towards me. As I clapped and hugged them gratefully before administering a couple of dog biscuits in reward, they reciprocated their gratitude by shaking half the contents of the River Ayr and its constituent tributaries all over my new white T-shirt, but I couldn't have cared less. I had my big dogs back again.

The next half hour or so was more or less completely incident-free. However, trust me, if I was ever given the opportunity to live my entire life all over again, I really would opt to enjoy that particular thirty-minute window a whole lot more, being as I was in complete and blissful ignorance of what was about to happen next.

As we followed the contours of the mighty river around a gentle S-bend, which then developed into a somewhat blind corner, Max stopped momentarily, sniffed the air again and took off like a bloody bullet. Cindy just looked at me.

'Don't just stand there gawking, Cindy,' I said. 'Go and see what he's up to this time.' And off she went again in hot pursuit.

When I turned the corner, I couldn't believe my eyes, and to be fair to Cindy, neither could she. There was Max, haring around one of the local farmer's grassy meadows, and giving chase to at least two dozen sheep. As the poor things darted eye-poppingly around in every single direction, Max bolted after each and every one of them in turn. They looked absolutely petrified, but probably no more so than Max's stand-in master, who had immediately clocked the possibility and associated irony of the farmer's own shotgun entering the equation.

I immediately climbed the fence that Max had obviously leapt over a few moments ago, and began running around like a bloody lunatic, but totally bereft of even the foggiest idea about what to do. My desperate response was all about action, but sadly lacking in strategy.

The whole chase must have lasted about three minutes all-in, by which time it had become apparent that Max had not the slightest intention of harming the sheep. He had just fancied a bit of a chase, that was all, and his frenetic energy levels were by now beginning to dissipate, thankfully slowing him down to a canter, and then to a mere trot. When he eventually slumped on the grass beside me with his tongue hanging out in exhaustion, it really was a sight for sore eyes. In sheer relief, I did what I should have done the moment we left the security of the car, which was to slip his leash over his big muscular neck.

'Right, you two,' I announced, as we continued along the footpath that contours the River Ayr. 'That has been quite enough drama for one day, thank you very much.'

Then I added sincerely, but rather foolishly as it would soon transpire, the following words of inspirational leadership. 'Max, my boy, this is your last chance.'

I took his leash off again. Big, big mistake. Monumental, in fact.

Little did I know at the time that the disappearing-dog trick and the sheep-terrorising act would prove to be mere trailers for the day's main feature, which was about to be beamed onto the screen of my disbelieving consciousness any moment now.

Everything was going fine, with both dogs weaving their various paths in-and-out of the lush waterside foliage, thus contriving to double their respective mileages in comparison to my own, when we came upon another sharp bend in the river. The footpath heralded yet another blind corner. Surely I had learned my lesson by now, hadn't I? Well no, actually.

With the intrepid Max leading the way, Cindy in semi-interested pursuit and yours truly plodding on behind and supposedly in charge of the proceedings, I turned the corner just in time to feel the need to bellow two frantic words.

'MAX, NO!'

Too late. By the time they had left my mouth, Max had already plunged from a height of at least eight or nine feet straight into the river, with an almighty 'S-P-L-A-A-S-S-H-H!'

causing an enormous cascade of waves to ripple outwards in a three-hundred-and-sixty-degree arc.

'I JUST DON'T BELIEVE IT!' I roared, throwing my hands up into the air.

'How the hell am I going to get you out of there?' I asked Max, simultaneously surveying the scene and immediately recognising that there was no obvious escape route, save for the near-vertical banking off which he had just plunged in scarcely-concealed abandon, a few seconds ago.

Then, just when I was beginning to think that things couldn't possibly get any worse, Cindy looked at me, and made a quite unforgettable pronouncement with her big intelligent eyes.

'Don't worry, we'll just have to use *Cindy Power*!' they announced confidently. 'I'll go and get him!'

As a blood-curdling yell of, 'CINDY, NO!' attempted to leave my already-strained vocal chords, she too leapt like a gazelle off the banking. She honestly must have hit the water at about fifty miles per hour.

Another almighty 'S-P-L-A-A-A-A-S-S-H-H!' assaulted my eardrums, and my mouth fell open again in utter disbelief. As a result of her sheer downward momentum, Cindy then completely disappeared from view beneath the water line, only for her big golden head to re-emerge a few moments later, at which point the two dogs started swimming and cavorting around beside each other in ever-decreasing circles, tails swishing merrily just beneath the surface and front paws patting playfully at each other. As I stood there in complete horror, it was obvious that neither Max nor Cindy had clocked the seriousness of the situation. They hadn't a bloody care in the world. They were having a ball.

I, on the other hand, was not.

As my aquatic canine companions continued to lunge around in the splendour of the River Ayr, I again surveyed the topography of the terrain that surrounded the big deep pool into which they had leapt with such carefree mirth. Upstream and to my left was a very fast-flowing section of the river that most certainly did not provide the answer, since it would have been quite impossible for them to swim up against such a strong current, even allowing for the fact that Labradors are extremely powerful swimmers. Directly underneath me was the cavernous pool in which they were still having such riotous fun, although rather worryingly, they were beginning to tire and slow down a bit by now. Between me and the pool was the steep, near-vertical banking, the ascent of which would have severely tested a seasoned Himalayan mountaineer. And to complete the doom-laden scenario, downstream was another abrupt bend in the riverbed, around which lay God-only-knows-what, but in these desperate circumstances, it looked like the only option worth trying.

By this time, Cindy had made her first attempt to jump out of the water and clamber up the steep, slippery mud-based banking, but only succeeded in slithering back down into the pool. Inevitably, Max then did likewise and ended up doing a flip backwards into the water beside her.

I looked at the expressions on both dogs' faces and, in particular, at the look in their eyes, both sets of which were beginning to radiate the first embryonic signs of panic.

'Aye, now you're beginning to realise the mess you've got us all into, aren't you?' I shouted at them, my voice a hybrid of exasperated anger and real concern. 'You pair of silly big bastards!'

The situation was becoming pretty serious by now, as both dogs tried time after time to climb the banking, only succeeding in slithering back into the water after every increasingly futile attempt. I had already established that there was no way I could walk in a downstream direction to coax them towards me, because the adjacent terrain and footpath had become much too high and distant from the river at that point.

I therefore concluded that desperate situations called for desperate measures. There was only one thing for it.

So I unlaced my walking boots, and chucked them behind a gorse bush. I then identified a big healthy-looking tree that overhung the banking, and fumbled around until I had located a branch strong enough to take my thirteen-and-a-half stones, after which I began my nervous descent. Thankfully, there was plenty of solid-looking vegetation all the way along the riverbank for me to grab onto, which was rather reassuring, in view of the fact that, to this very day, I cannot swim a single stroke to save myself. The complete folly of my actions was not lost on me, but I simply could never have stood there watching Cindy and Max panic and, God forbid, perish.

As soon as I slipped my body into the water, the cold hit me. It was bloody freezing, autumn or not. The dogs swam towards me, tails swishing ecstatically, and tongues licking my face in gratitude for their deeply misguided master joining the party.

'If we're gonna go, we're gonna go together!' I announced much more cheerily than I felt, let me assure you.

'Let's try to swim downstream and see what's round this bloody corner.'

As I slowly-but-surely shuffled my semi-submerged frame in the direction of the current that was, rather worryingly, much heavier underneath the water line than it appeared on the surface, by virtue of grabbing successive handfuls of lush-green foliage on the banking, Cindy and Max swam behind me like a pair of new-born ducklings following obediently in their mother's wake. When we painstakingly turned the corner, I just closed my eyes and prayed silently for some sign of a possible escape route, because there was literally no way back, given the strength of the current.

When I opened them again, I simply couldn't believe our luck, as I saw the river develop into a comparatively shallow stream. A few minutes later and I was literally walking through the water at no more than knee-height, with both dogs half-swimming, half-lunging in grateful pursuit. The only residual problem was the sheer incline of the massive banking to our right that led, hopefully, back to the footpath, but we would cope. Give me a lung-bursting climb up a steep hillside instead of a lung-filled watery grave any day, I remember thinking to myself.

Ten minutes later, I had collected my boots again, and another forty minutes after that, the three of us were sitting squelching our way home in the Capri.

'Don't say a thing, Cindy,' I dared her, as I caught her humiliated glance in the rear-view mirror. 'Not a bloody word.'

She just smacked her lips, turned her head away from my scolding gaze and curled up beside the again-shivering Max.

'And Nan never finds out. Got it?'

I took her silence as an affirmative.

When Andy and Susan returned on the Monday evening to reunite themselves with their darling black Labrador, Susan asked how things had gone, as Max licked both their faces in unadulterated glee.

'It was all pretty uneventful, really,' replied Nan. Cindy and I just looked at each other.

'Mum's the word,' Cindy's eyes said sheepishly.

Saving Bertie

'It isn't the mountains ahead to climb that wear you out;
it's the pebble in your shoe.'
(Muhammad Ali, former world heavyweight boxing champion)

As a happy consequence of Cindy's wise counsel that, for purely practical reasons, Nan really needed to start using a wheelchair rather than contorting her entire skeletal frame around on a pair of wooden walking sticks, and of my painfully protracted but ultimately successful efforts to persuade her to do just that, my still twenty-something wife happened upon another unexpected bonus. She actually learned to drive a car again.

I had delved into a few topical articles on such relatively modern gadgets for disabled drivers as customised hand controls, these being ingeniously deigned to fit onto the steering columns of 'ordinary' vehicles equipped with fully automatic gearboxes, which rendered the driver capable of operating the car without the requirement for once-athletic but now hopelessly non-functional legs having to play any part whatsoever. Thus, within a very short period of time since Cindy's words of wisdom, Nan could now propel herself independently in her wheelchair towards her new car, into which she could then scramble rather inelegantly, and drive away at breakneck speed with yet more new-found independence.

The initial stigma proved very difficult indeed for Nan, particularly in relation to the use of her recently acquired, but very heavy and cumbersome wheelchair. However, through time, life on wheels would prove to be completely revolutionary. (Just where do I get these unintentional puns from, I often wonder? I suppose it must be some kind of unwelcome gift, although I'd much prefer having the ability to bend teaspoons without even touching them.)

Anyway, as a very agreeable result of Nan's new found mobility and much enhanced independence, the family found its way onto the Ardrossan-to-Brodick ferry one Saturday morning in early July, *en route* to the idyllic little island of Arran, which lies majestically just off the south-west coast of Scotland. Arran had held a very special place in our hearts since our respective childhoods, and would go on in later years to become our personal sanctuary and, ultimately, our home. However, our visit to the island in 1982 would prove to be a watershed for the family, in terms of assorted sets of wheels having provided us – and Nan in particular - with a new and terribly exciting lease of life.

As I stood on the deck of the *MV Clansman* beside six-year-old Jillian and her eighteen-month-old brother Derek, Nan sat imprisoned three floors below us in the driver's seat of our Ford Cortina, which was located in the vessel's cavernous car deck, with nine-year-old Cindy beside her on the passenger's seat. When the ship's mighty engines cranked into life, Cindy sprang onto Nan's knee, pinning her against the back of the seat like a wrestler trying to hold down his latest opponent on a three-count. Cindy was never one for acclimatising easily to strange new procedures, particularly when her lord-and-master wasn't on hand to speak to her reassuringly in *Dogmanese*.

In the event, our fortnight on Arran turned out to be absolutely wonderful in every regard, and transpired to give the family new hope that life for all of us could still be a very exciting prospect indeed, despite the earlier hideous intrusion of a horrible, debilitating disease that had tried its utmost to wreck Nan's own.

However, while my ageing brain still retains many very fond memories of that wonderful holiday on the sunshine isle, one particular event will stay with me for ever, and in no small way as a result of the great pride I felt for Cindy on that occasion.

One evening after the family had spent most of the day exploring the delightful south side of the island by car, with Nan having driven the whole way, while the two kids, Cindy and myself participated in all sorts of exciting treks in the woods and playful cavortings along the sandy beaches, we retired to our local pub for a bar meal with another family we had met earlier in the week, and who would go on to become lifelong friends. It was during an overheard conversation between the barman and a clearly distraught middle-aged lady, that we soon became aware of the reason for the latter's obvious dismay. Being unable to resist the intrigue, and having clocked that it had something to do with a lost dog, I eventually managed to wriggle my big gob into the conversation.

Basically the dear woman, whose husband had tragically passed away only a few months back, had been out rambling in the hills that afternoon with her rather elderly King Charles spaniel called Bertie and, quite inexplicably, the poor old gent had wandered off into the ferns and gone missing. After a few increasingly frenetic hours of searching, the lady had eventually scrambled back down the hillside in a bit of a stew, to the island's main village of Brodick, where she had enlisted the assistance of a few friends and volunteers, who had then willingly joined her to look for the intrepid Bertie. Unfortunately, all had returned empty-handed and pretty despondent, as darkness began to descend over the heather-clad slopes.

The poor lady was beside herself with anxiety. The barman and a few of the locals had tried to reassure her that in view of the lovely summer weather we were having, and the readily available fresh water supplies from the numerous mountain streams, her wee dog would be in no immediate danger overnight. However, she was having none of it. Somebody bought her another gin-and-tonic, which she immediately necked with shaking hands, before heading home in a terrible state.

When I crawled out of bed the next morning, I sincerely hoped that the unfortunate woman had enjoyed a better sleep than I had, because I simply didn't get a bloody wink, having tossed and turned all through the night just thinking about the wee geriatric Bertie scurrying frantically hither and thither in forlorn search of his beloved mistress.

'Fancy a wee bit of mountain rescue this morning?' I asked Cindy, as she licked the last remaining morsels of her tinned dog food off her chin.

'What are you on about?' she replied with a quizzical expression, so I explained the situation to her.

Half an hour later, I had parked the car at the top of the Lamlash brae, and we began marching up the well-worn footpath towards Clauchlands Hill, the scene of the distraught lady's last sighting of her beloved Bertie. Ever the optimist, I had draped Cindy's spare and more threadbare lead around my neck, intertwining it with the lovely bright red one that Santa had given her the previous Christmas.

When we reached the top of the hill, we stopped temporarily to take in the magnificent panorama before us. To our left was the semi-circular Brodick Bay, into which the *MV Clansman* was once more making its way, this time to convert itself into the 11.05 ferry back to Ardrossan on the mainland, to transport those unfortunate souls who were having to leave the island's splendour that particular day. Straight ahead in the background lay the entire Ayrshire coastline, while some sixty degrees to my right and in the immediate foreground sprawled the sinister but beautiful Holy Isle, just off Lamlash Bay.

It was the unusual sound of people chattering in the normally silent hillside foliage that broke my trance. There were about a dozen of them walking around the heather and ferns, and scrambling through the parallel lines of pine trees, obviously still searching for the little spaniel, who had probably not enjoyed his most comfortable night, if indeed he was still alive to tell the tale. I informed the group of volunteers that I would try my luck a bit further on, postulating that the wee dog might well have wandered off in the pitch darkness, in the diametrically opposite direction to that from which his mistress had originally brought him.

'Oh well, if you think so,' the lady's younger sister had replied. It was hardly an encouraging response, but I had figured that widening our coverage was at least worth a try, since there was probably little that another pair of eager searchers could meaningfully do in an area already populated by a dozen increasingly fretting incumbents.

When we reached the top of the next peak, I parked my backside on a large boulder, and Cindy sat down on the grass beside me, both of us staring out to sea.

'What do you think, Cindy?' I asked her, my voice probably radiating as much concerned indecision as I was feeling. 'This is your territory, lass, so I'm looking for a wee bit of inspiration.'

She just looked at me without reply, then raised her big black snout skywards, and sniff-sniff-sniffed the mid-morning air. 'Let's go this way,' her eyes suggested, more in hope than certainty I imagined.

And off she went like a bullet, straight down the long, steep track towards the wooden fence and stile that were designed to encourage the island's many ramblers to head either left for Brodick, or right for Lamlash. By this time, Cindy's body language was beginning to take on a more deeply focused appearance, and her energy levels were clearly escalating.

As Cindy leapt the fence I shouted, 'Wait for me!' and clambered rather less stylishly over the stile, wondering which of the two directions she would choose. To my surprise she chose neither, and began scampering up the steep hillside straight ahead that leads to Dun Fion, an ancient iron-age fort perched at the top of a mound from which indigenous warriors once threw sticks and stones at would-be assailants, to repel them from invading this precious little island.

'CINDY, COME HERE!' I commanded, as I plodded breathlessly up the steep incline, with my charge almost at the summit by this time. She stopped in her tracks, took stock of the situation, and just stood there looking rather irritated by this sudden reversal of momentum.

'CINDY, COME HERE!' I said again, more firmly this time and deploying the associated hand gesture, at which point she trotted back down the hill to my side, sheer annoyance still radiating from her face. The thing was that I had literally no idea why she had decided to run in that particular direction, since for all I knew, she might just have fancied the spectacular view at the top. There again, I reminded myself as I scratched my stubble-clad chin, of the three possible options, this one was certainly the most taxing, so what exactly was she up to?

'Could you possibly tell me where we are we going, Cindy?' I asked her. 'If it's not too much trouble, that is.' She didn't even look at me.

Cindy's body language was all over the place, by this time. Her skeletal gait was absolutely stalk-still, her tail was as rigid as a fireside poker, her ears twitched continuously and her nostrils dilated-and-contracted repetitively with blistering rapidity in the direction from which she had been commanded to return which, into the bargain, happened to be downwind as well as uphill. However, it was the look in her eyes that said it all. Her pupils were absolutely enormous. Quite simply, Cindy was 'in the zone', to use the modern parlance.

'Cindy, where the bloody hell are we going?' I repeated. Try though I might, I just couldn't get her attention.

'Right then, WAY OUT!' I shouted, in the resigned realisation that she was now most certainly on a mission, whatever that mission might transpire to be. My guess was that she had sniffed out a couple of hares, rabbits or whatever. My hope, however, was that the same nostrils had located a severely disorientated, elderly Charlie spaniel.

Up the hill she bolted again towards Dun Fion, with her bewildered master panting his ascent in her frenetic slipstream. I remembered with a bit of a shudder, from one earlier such jaunt, that the northerly face of the hill presented a cavernous drop of some three hundred metres or so, onto some huge rocks below, which themselves lay only another couple of hundred metres from the sea. I prayed that Cindy would have the experience and common sense not to go plunging over the edge in a fit of blind enthusiasm.

At that point, three booming barks erupted from her mighty lungs. The very distinctive, 'WOW! WOW! WOW!' represented only one thing. Nan and I always called it her 'serious bark'. On this particular occasion, I realised that Cindy meant business.

When I had eventually dragged my weary, hyperventilating frame to the summit, the views of the Firth of Clyde were as breathtaking as my hill-climbing efforts had been only a few moments previously. However, we hadn't come all this way to admire the bloody scenery, I reminded myself.

Another, 'WOW! WOW! WOW!' assaulted my eardrums through the warm, whistling south-westerly breeze.

'What is it, lass?' I asked her expectantly, and marched over to where she was standing, as fast as my now-aching limbs could carry me. Thankfully, that was towards the southerly and much more gentle slope of the hillside, an observation that was not lost on me as I saw Cindy beginning her descent over the horizon.

'CINDY, STAY!' I shouted, then repeated the command. Like the good dog she was, she stayed put.

When I reached her side, I peered over the edge. And there to my indescribable relief was a rather bedraggled-looking little dog lying at the foot of the slope, against a wire fence, with its tail wagging. I immediately concluded that, if he wasn't Bertie, it would sure be one hell of a coincidence to have two different King Charles Spaniels lost on the same hillside on the same day.

'CINDY, WAY OUT!' I shouted, at which point she absolutely thundered down the hillside towards her new-found canine colleague, her own tail swishing furiously to counter-balance her momentum against the numerous undulations of the slope, but also signalling her bursting eagerness to make the poor little fellow's acquaintance.

As I scrambled my own way down the hillside, I began to notice that the spaniel's body wasn't really moving all that much, save for his head and tail, and I began to wonder if the unfortunate little fellow had broken a leg, or suffered some other similar serious misfortune.

'BERTIE!' I shouted, as I continued my descent, and his little tail began to oscillate like a supercharged metronome. 'Bertie, we're coming to get you, son!'

By this time, Cindy had well-and-truly introduced herself to Bertie, having sniffed every single square centimetre of his matted coat, the prostrate little chap just lying there and luxuriating in the female touch. When I eventually reached him, I stroked his forehead very gently and began talking to him as reassuringly as I could in the circumstances, while Cindy continued with her oral exploration.

And that was when I clocked why Bertie wasn't moving. The poor little bugger had caught his hind leg in the wire mesh of the fence, most probably trying to wriggle through it in the pitch blackness of an extremely stressful night. I shuddered when I thought of the sheer horror of the situation in which the unfortunate thing must have found himself.

Thankfully, he allowed me to fiddle about with the mesh, which I fairly quickly disentangled from his back leg with the aid of the penknife I always carry with me when I'm roaming the hills, but not before I had slipped the spare leash over his neck, in case he decided to make a bolt for freedom, once released. Within a couple of minutes, he was walking by my side, albeit rather gingerly, and Cindy was cavorting around in ecstasy, like a Brazilian striker who had just scored the winning goal in the last minute of the World Cup Final.

To avoid the need for further climbing, we simply plodded through the waist-high grass, thus circumscribing the foot of Dun Fion, which took us back to the stile, over which I literally carried the truly-knackered Bertie, as Cindy again decided to show off by springing over the fence like one of the many indigenous deer. She was truly in her element. 'Am I not just the cleverest dog in the world?' her still saucer-like eyes appeared to say.

Realising that the bedraggled little chap had probably had nothing to eat or drink for a very long time, I took a slight detour towards a nearby hillside stream, from which Bertie drank copiously for a good minute or so. He then willingly accepted a handful of dog biscuits from my trouser pocket, while the temporarily non-plussed Cindy got only one, but she would cope.

Within ten minutes or so, we came upon some of the rescue party who were still meandering around rather despondently in the lush ferns. When they spotted wee Bertie trotting by my side on a lead, they all swished their way as fast as their legs could carry them through the heavy foliage towards us in sheer relief. To this day, I will never forget the tears of joy that ran down his mistress's cheeks, when she cradled in her arms the little bundle of joy that she thought she would never, ever see again.

'Thank you! Thank you! Thank you!' she wept, hugging me and grabbing my arm in a vice-like grip.

'Don't thank me. Thank Cindy!' I replied with a beaming grin, gesticulating to the golden heroine perched proudly at my feet. 'It was Cindy who found Bertie, not me.'

'Oh Cindy!' she gasped, and draped her shaking body around the heroine of the hour. 'What a clever dog you are! Would you like a biscuit?'

Hands still trembling on account of the adrenalin that continued to course through her veins, she then proceeded to bring out from her anorak pocket a plastic bag full of dog biscuits which, almost predictably, she then succeeded in dropping onto the grass. Cindy grabbed the whole bag and buggered off into the woods.

'This mountain rescue is hungry work, you know!' her still-beaming eyes announced, from a very safe distance.

The whole hillside roared in laughter.

A Christmas Cracker

'The dog was created especially for children. He is the God of Frolic.'
(Henry Ward Beecher, Social Reformist)

My alarm clock beep-beep-beeped, but it needn't have bothered.

The kids were already up on our bed, bouncing about on top of Nan and me, such that continued sleep would have been a physical impossibility. A mighty, booming bark came from the direction of downstairs, immediately followed by another one, then two more, and finally came the unmistakeable sound of canine claws scratching on varnished wood.

'Go and let Cindy out of the kitchen, or she'll soon have the whole damned place dismantled,' I said to them, rubbing my weary eyes. They both immediately jumped off the bed and bounded down the stairs, two-at-a-time, in uncharacteristic but willing compliance.

I looked at the clock. It was seven-thirty, and much too early to rise on a day off work. However, the twenty-fifth of December was no ordinary holiday. Nan turned towards me and kissed me on the lips. 'Merry Christmas, light of my life!'

'Merry Christmas to you too' I mumbled sleepily, pecking her gently on the cheek.

The very instant the kitchen door opened, all hell broke loose, as two human and two canine pairs of feet burst along the hall and thundered up the stairs.

'OH NO!' Nan shouted, and dived under the duvet, a mere nanosecond before Cindy sprang from a distance of about two metres straight onto the bed. As she began licking my face, and scratching feverishly at the bedclothes to locate Nan's and deliver a similar saliva-laden administration, Jillian and Derek screamed in pure delight and unbridled excitement.

'Can we go down and open our presents?' gasped Jillian, her big blue eyes radiating the sheer joy that heralds an eight-year-old's Christmas morning. 'Now, Daddy? Please? Please?'

'Please! Please! Please! Please! Please!' shouted Derek, aged three, but about to turn four in one week's time.

'Right now! Right now! Right now!' he continued yelling, using my still-slumbering body as a trampoline. It was the final bounce that really woke me up, his little foot crash-landing straight onto my unprotected groin.

'OOOOH, MY BOLLOCKS!' I groaned, and the kids shrieked in mischievous delight.

A few minutes later, four of us were prancing around in joyous anticipation and unbearable suspense immediately outside the living room door, behind which we just knew for sure that Santa Claus would already have deposited our assorted presents in exchange for a cup of tea, a digestive biscuit and a supermarket carrot for the loyal Rudolph. However, it would be at least another couple of minutes before the ceremonial door-opening could take place, since Nan still required to bump-bump-bump her backside down the remaining eleven stairs, having thus far negotiated only the first six.

By the time the whole family had eventually burst into the living room in a mad wave of frenzied excitement, we had all anticipated that the day would doubtless be notable for many reasons, but none of us had the foggiest idea that it would be absolutely memorable for one in particular. Christmas day, 1984, which also happened to be Cindy's eleventh birthday, was about to go down in folklore as her most manic. And trust me, that's saying something.

The canine performance from hell began to materialise almost immediately the kids dived into several kilometres of wrapping paper. Now, I honestly cannot remember the detail of who-gave-what-to-whom on that particular Christmas morning, save for Nan presenting me with a *Deep Purple* album and yours truly reciprocating with yet another *Abba* offering to her, but I do have vivid memories of the children's favourite presents, principally because of their reactions when they first saw them.

Jillian's eyes widened like saucers as soon as she spied her favourite *Muppet* character, the ultra-green and decidedly hideous Kermit the Frog, sitting perched cheekily on a cosy little chocolate-brown settee that we had procured for a tenner out of the local hardware store.

'K-E-R-M-I-T-T-T!' she screamed, as she bolted across the living room floor. A second or two later, she was sitting proudly on her cheap settee with Kermit cradled in her left arm, her right thumb and forefinger in her mouth and the happiest, most contented smile I have ever had the pleasure to witness.

'T-R-A-A-A-C-T-T-T-O-R-R-R-R-R-R!' croaked her younger brother, almost unable to breathe in pure excitement, as he spotted a miniature but surprisingly realistic replica of his very favourite contraption on earth, as many a hyperactive car journey along Ayrshire's myriad of rural farm roads had already testified.

So there we all were, as deliriously happy as it is possible to be in this life, with Jillian on her soft toy settee cuddling an ugly cloth frog in her lap, Derek sitting on his toy tractor roaring out his various 'Brm Brm Brms', and their proud mum and dad admiring the covers and playlists of our new and mercifully quite different albums. Meanwhile, Cindy was chomping feverishly on the contents of a doggy selection box, whilst simultaneously rummaging through the Christmas wrapping paper for more such gastric delights.

And then, all of a sudden, she turned to face me. I could see it in her eyes, as I had done so many times before, and it was completely unmistakable. Pure unadulterated mischief.

'CINDY, NO!' I roared at her, having not the remotest idea about what she was about to do, but in the absolutely certain knowledge that she was going to do it.

And in that instant, she took two steps and sprang through

the air with an almighty leap that totally belied her eleven years, and grabbed a bright-red bauble that had been hanging innocently from the second-top branch of our seven-foot-high Christmas tree, crash-landing on top of our teak coffee table and sending a crystal vase spinning on its way to complete atomisation against the big bay window, which immediately shattered in synchronised empathy. The whole thing seemed to play itself out in some sort of surreal slow motion action sequence.

No sooner had my disbelieving eyes begun to make sense of what had just happened, than the Christmas tree then began to collapse in the wake of the sheer momentum of Cindy's acrobatic leap, like a huge forest pine being felled by a burly lumberjack's mighty axe, and plunged over the mesmerised little heads of Jillian and Derek, both of whom had been sitting contentedly on couch and tractor respectively. By the time the dust had settled, the chill December air was whistling in through the bay window and the kids were invisible.

If the high-flying, bauble-grabbing act had only taken a few seconds, then the clean-up process, complete with a hefty smack on the arse for Cindy, took at least half an hour. Into the bargain, my pathetic attempts to board up the shattered window were only rewarded around lunchtime when my dear neighbour Stewart, himself a frustrated would-be carpenter, had eventually to be summonsed and beseeched to save what was left of our Christmas day.

Meanwhile, Nan was doing her stuff in the kitchen to make Christmas dinner for the invited guests, which comprised our immediate family and a few special friends. The menu was a very tried-and-tested one, consisting of a starter of smoked salmon salad, a main course of roast turkey with all the trimmings, and a dessert of Christmas pudding and brandy butter completing the three-course feast. Hardly an original formula, but superbly cooked and wonderfully presented by Nan. As always.

When our guests arrived to admire the children's presents

and our new plywood window pane, my job was to keep them going with assorted alcoholic beverages in order to whet their appetites and further stimulate their playfulness, thereby ensuring that the customary yuletide mirth would be cranked up to maximum volume. Meanwhile, I helped Nan out in the kitchen as and when required, with certain chores that were rather more difficult for her to perform unaided, in the context of her own physical limitations, like putting crockery and cutlery on the table, taking the turkey out of the oven and so on. Nan then placed the starters on the table, and came through to the living room to join us in a well-earned refreshment of vodka-and-fresh orange.

As we all sat chatting, the adults playing with Jillian, Derek and their multitudinous toys, Nan's mum uttered just two innocent little words.

'Where's Cindy?'

In an instant, that all-too-familiar feeling of complete dread hit me again.

'Oh no!' I said quietly, then turned and stared anxiously at Nan.

'THE BLOODY SALMON!' she gasped, throwing her hands up over her head in complete horror.

I shot along the hall, both children behind me as it transpired, and into the dining room, just in time to see Cindy standing with her hind legs on one of the chairs and her front paws on the table, necking the very last one of the nine helpings of Loch Fyne smoked salmon.

'CINDY, YOU GREEDY BASTARD!' I screeched, totally unaware that the kids were there beside me by this time.

They immediately began howling in laughter, and not just at Cindy's act of complete wickedness, but no doubt also at their school-teacher-father's impressive command of the vernacular. As Cindy shot off the chair for dear life, her new bright-blue Christmas collar caught on the white lace tablecloth that a work colleague had given us for a wedding present some twelve years back, and she then somehow contrived to haul the dining room table's entire contents onto the floor with an almighty crash, as she sped out of the kitchen and up the stairs for dear life.

I immediately sprinted after her, leaping three steps at a time, only to find her curled up in a ball under the double bed, where she knew from similar past experience that I could not get hold of her. By the time I eventually cajoled her to come out, I had managed to calm down, the guests were all in hysterics, the dining room table had been neatly rearranged and everyone was sitting down to their reconstituted two-course meal.

'Would you like another drink, Ian?' my dear wife enquired, attempting in vain to hold back her laughter. Everyone else exploded in hysterical unison. I looked down at my feet, and there was the inimitable Cindy sitting next to them. The saliva dripped expectantly from her mouth onto my new Christmas boots and, very tentatively, she gave me a paw.

'I'd like my main course now,' her big eyes said to me.

Three further incidents contrived to characterise Cindy's epic performance on that manic, but absolutely wonderful Christmas day all those years ago. Firstly, as the whole family moved back through to the living room to massage swelling tummies and participate in an assortment of dubious board games whilst sipping various beverages to the strains of *Abba* in their pomp (I was only ever permitted to listen to *Deep Purple* through my headphones, you see), Cindy decided that it would be a good idea to give Kermit the Frog a serious humping in full view of all in attendance.

Then, about half an hour later, as if to attempt to bring our own sex life to the top of the agenda, she came skipping down the stairs and into the living room, where she deposited a two-dozen box of condoms at Nan's mum's feet.

Her crowning glory came, however, after a manic half-hour of chasing, and being chased, by the kids. As she sat by my side, panting feverishly with her tongue hanging out and nearly touching the floor, she decided that the time was right to vomit into my malt-whisky-and-soda. That did it.

'RIGHT CINDY, GO TO BED!' I commanded, and she complied instantly.

An hour or so later, Jillian and Derek followed suit almost voluntarily, as a consequence of their utter exhaustion, after which the rest of our guests left too, deeply satisfied with the glorious Christmas fare, the human company and the canine mischievousness. Once Nan and I had done the washing up and got the house back into some kind of order, she bumped her weary posterior back up our seventeen stairs to get ready for bed and drift effortlessly into a well-earned sleep.

Meanwhile, I sat on the kitchen floor and decided to have a little word with Cindy, who was curled up in her own bed. Her big sleepy eyes were the first to break the visual silence.

'I've been a bad dog today, haven't I?' they enquired rhetorically.

'You've been a complete little bastard, Cindy,' I replied. 'And allow me to tell you why,' I continued.

'Since you got up this morning, you have managed to fell the Christmas tree, break an expensive crystal vase, disintegrate a window pane, bury the kids under a pile of pine needles, baubles and flashing lights, eat nine helpings of smoked salmon, fornicate with a toy frog, inform my mother-in-law that Nan and I intend to screw each other at least another twenty-four times and, to put the tin lid on your behaviour today, you then decided to end with your party trick of spewing your guts up into my Glenfiddich malt whisky.'

'But it's Christmas,' she replied rather pathetically.

'Your point being?' I asked with a supercilious frown.

'That I'm supposed to enjoy myself. Everybody else laughed at me too. And everybody was happy. We're all supposed to be happy at Christmas, aren't we?'

'Yes we are, Cindy. Yes we are.'

'And it's my birthday too,' she added. 'I'm eleven today.'

'So what's that got to do with it, I wonder?' I asked smugly.

'Because I might not have many more Christmases and birthdays left,' she said.

I cradled my beloved ten-quid puppy's head in my arms and kissed her on the nose, as the tears began streaming down my cheeks.

Words of Wisdom

'*Courage is the art of being the only one who knows you're scared to death.*'
(*Harold Wilson, former British Prime Minister*)

Cindy's fourteenth birthday coincided with my elevation into school management, as Assistant Head Teacher in an Ayrshire secondary school that was even further away from home than my previous place of employment. Not only was my travelling time now further extended, but the additional responsibilities of the job simply contrived to make my working day even longer still.

However, Nan and I had discussed the situation prior to my decision to apply for the post, and we had decided that my promotion, should it transpire, would be good for the family in two senses. Firstly, it was patently obvious to everyone who knew me that I was really excited about the prospect of moving onto the next stage of my career, and secondly, it would give us that little bit of additional financial security in our lives. Like most families in which one of the adults is disabled, we were a one-wage team and our finances could become a wee bit stretched at times. Allied to that, Nan had built up a fairly comprehensive social infrastructure around her by this time, with family, friends, local shopkeepers and the like making sure that my wonderful family would be denied neither sustenance nor recreation, while I was temporarily unavailable to perform these basic tasks, on account of being out toiling to earn corn for the table.

However, and crucially, I had also discussed the whole thing in advance with Cindy, and it was she who had told me to stop fretting and just go for it. I'll never forget our conversation one sunny-but-breezy spring afternoon, while we were sitting on a wooded hillside in the magnificent grounds of Ayrshire's majestic Culzean Castle, which overlooks the Firth of Clyde, with our beloved island of Arran across the sea as a spectacular backdrop.

As we rested there, my own backside parked on a felled tree trunk and Cindy lying loyally by my side as usual, I reminisced for a few moments on the momentous treks we used to embark upon when she was younger and in her physical pomp. I remembered the days of chasing her around the beach when she was a puppy, and laughed out loud as I recalled the summer's afternoon when, to her shock and consternation, she accidentally somersaulted backwards all the way down a steep hillside, simply because she had been staring at a picnicker's cheese sandwich instead of noticing the sharp incline a foot or so behind her. I thought of her glorious golden head, her dark ears, her silky tail and her jet-black nose, all features defining a picture of health, happiness and zest.

That afternoon, however, we had walked only a mile or so along Maidens beach and Cindy was pretty well exhausted. As she lay panting at my feet, I looked at the greying whiskers, the yellowing teeth and the once-golden, now-fading fleece, and shuddered at the thought that the good lord who had blessed me with her glorious companionship would surely, some day soon, take her away from me again. How would I ever cope without my big dog?

At that moment, Cindy scrambled a bit unsteadily onto her feet, and sat between my legs, staring out to sea. She just instinctively knew that some dark thought or other had begun cascading its pernicious way through my hyperactive mind. After all, she always did know what I was thinking.

I wriggled my backside off the big tree trunk, and lay down beside her in the early spring ferns. She turned and looked at me, then licked my face. It was at that point that I noticed something quite remarkable, and very reassuring into the bargain. If most of her more obvious physical characteristics were rapidly ageing and deteriorating, her big bright eyes remained exactly the same as those which first hypnotised me on that awful day at Dalblair Bridge. Cindy's body was certainly showing the tell-tale signs of wear and tear, but for some strange reason, her eyes seemed to have retained their youthfulness.

The truth of the matter is that I had already read up on a bit of research about the canine ageing process and, to be perfectly honest, all it had achieved was to make me fret, and to question exactly why I seemed so hell-bent on continually putting myself through such traumas. Especially for someone who has such a ridiculously vivid imagination, and an infuriating propensity to establish worst-case-scenarios in every single situation, I reminded myself.

And so I learned that, as dogs get older, not only do some of their more obvious physical attributes begin to deteriorate in terms of appearance and performance, but so too does their capacity to transmit, receive and process important information. The actual rate of deterioration varies enormously across the various canine breeds, and indeed from dog to dog within each breed. However, a number of environmental and lifestyle factors can influence their quality of physical and emotional lives as they continue to age. In short, the more active elderly dogs are in body and in mind, the better their chances of physiological and psychological longevity tend to be. So I resolved to take Cindy a decent walk every day for as long as she could manage it. I even thought about buying a year's supply of crossword books for her to sail through, as she lay in her bed recovering after her exertions, but then realised that this might be taking things a bit too far.

However, what had really worried me was the research evidence suggesting that dogs' eyesight also begins to deteriorate significantly as they get older, mainly on account of the constituent parts of their eyes losing a bit of strength and elasticity. The sad result is that older dogs begin to see life increasingly through a kind of mist, and unfortunately spectacles are not really all that practical an option.

However, Cindy's eyes still seemed to present in exactly the same fashion as they had done throughout her whole life, at least to her increasingly anxious master. The intelligence, the interest and the sparkle were still there, make no mistake. Yet, sadly, now circumscribing them were the wispy-yellowing fur, the once-black-now-beige nose and the rapidly-greying beard. It was as if the youthfulness of her piercing eyes had been cryogenically suspended in time, encased in an ever-ageing, but still magnificent head.

'You're not getting any younger lass, are you?' I asked, smiling at her a bit apprehensively.

'And neither are you!' her big eyes retorted impudently. 'You're thirty-eight, and I'm only fourteen. Remember?'

'Aye, but that's seventy in dog years, Cindy,' I added ruefully.

'Look, I'll be around for a wee while yet, so don't get all broody on me. I'm not past my sell-by date quite yet, you know.'

'I know,' I said to her, fully aware that she was just being brave for both of us, but equally cognizant of the approaching imminence of her inescapable departure from the life we had both shared together for so many years.

'Right, snap out of it!' she said.

I looked into her eyes. If her retinal rods and cones were knackered, as indeed they were supposed to be by now, they could have bloody fooled me. The devilment was still there, the mischief and the fun, if admittedly not quite in such ebullient proportions as they once had been. 'Maturity at long last', was what Nan and I had put it all down to.

'Snap out of what?' I replied, all defensive.

'This nonsense about me popping my clogs. You're not getting rid of me that easily.'

'Right, you've made your point, Cindy,' I conceded. 'So what is it you want to tell me, because I know you've got something on your mind. I can see it in your eyes, so cough up.'

'You need to think about the future, Ian,' she told me, completely out of the blue and to my astonishment. 'You need to think about where your life is going, about making things easier for Nan, and about what's best for Jillian and Derek.'

'So what do I need to do then, smart-arse?' I enquired, rather nervously.

'You know exactly what you need to do,' she replied with the merest twinkle in her eye.

'So you're trying to tell me that we need to leave our beautiful home, aren't you Cindy?' I exclaimed, rather irritated. 'It's been the only home we've ever known. Every single memory I have of Nan, the kids and you, Cindy, are in that house.'

Cindy's pupils narrowed and her mouth closed, her face taking on her 'serious' expression, as we used to call it

'Nan is really struggling, Ian. She has to shuffle up and down the stairs on her backside every single day in life, she can only use about half of the rooms in the house, and she can't even get out into the garden any more.'

So I replied, in a fit of pique, 'And just how am I going to pay for this new house then, Cindy?'

'By applying for that job!' she snapped. 'And by making bloody sure you get it!'

I was completely startled, but it really was the message I had wanted to hear all along.

'Okay then, genius. And how will you feel about moving home, after all these years?' I asked a bit impishly.

'I won't be coming with you, Ian,' she replied ruefully. 'You'll have to go without me. And you must get another dog. Promise me.'

I just stared at her, not knowing what to say, or what to think. My head was all over the place. I started to panic.

'Cindy, how could I ever get by without you?' I blurted out, my eyes beginning to glaze over. 'You have been everything to me. My best friend, my personal mentor, my ....well, my wonderful big dog. I just don't know how I'd ever manage on my own.'

'You will never be on your own,' she said through her piercing eyes, 'because I'll always be there.'

'I don't understand, Cindy,' I said, blinking a few tears away.

'I know you don't, Ian,' she replied, smiling through the

warmth of her eyes. 'And you mere human beings never will!'

'So how will I know when you're "there", when you've, ...
well, when you've left me?' I asked anxiously.

'Because I just will be,' she replied reassuringly, sporting one
of her knowing little smiles. 'After all, I have always been there
for you, haven't I big man?

I just stared at her, completely befuddled about the whole
conversation, as I blew my nose into a paper hankie. And it was
then that she dropped the bombshell.

'I was even there for you on your first day at secondary
school,' she said. 'You called me Meg. Remember?'

My jawbone landed on the sand.

The Elixir Of Life

'Age wrinkles the body. Quitting wrinkles the soul.'
(Douglas MacArthur, American General, World War II)

Cindy's words on that remarkable spring day proved to be prophetic. In the sense that we must never take anything for granted, that is, and certainly not our dubious right to longevity.

The ensuing early winter months turned out to be rather harsh and, save for a few sporadic days being blown on tiptoe along Ayr beach and one or two others battling over the local fields into the vicious teeth of northerly icy gales, Cindy and I never really ventured all that far from Cumnock's splendid Woodroad and Broomfield parks. The appalling weather was the main reason for our self-imposed anaerobic parochialism, but the reluctant acceptance of Cindy's advancing years was another.

By that time, her entire metabolism had begun to slow down quite noticeably, and it soon became apparent that the halcyon days of trekking the fifteen miles from nearby Muirkirk's Cairn Table – a rather flattish mountain from the summit of which one can enjoy a spectacular, three-hundred-and-sixty-degree panoramic view of the beautiful Ayrshire countryside – to the market town of Sanquhar in neighbouring Dumfriesshire, were well and truly over.

No, nowadays, a half-mile stroll down to one of the local parks, or a quiet swim in the Afton Water were all that my beloved Cindy could really manage by that time, and even those relatively modest exertions still left her panting breathlessly on most occasions. Nevertheless, she was still enjoying life, albeit at a much more leisurely pace, and she seemed to derive great pleasure and quiet satisfaction from simply lying on the living room carpet and observing the antics of Jillian and Derek as they continued to grow and develop. For Cindy, people-watching was always a completely fascinating activity, most probably on account of her superbly well-developed cognitive powers.

Then one day the following March, everything changed in an instant. I came home from work about half-past five as usual, to the customary greetings from Nan and the children. After sipping a coffee and cajoling Jillian and, in particular Derek to get their homework done before dinner, I found myself wondering why Cindy was not welded to my armchair as usual.

'Cindy!' I shouted. Nothing.

'Cindy, come on lass!' Still nothing. Not a sound.

'Nan, where is she?' I enquired of the cook in the kitchen, a bit more anxiously by that time.

'She's just lying in her bed,' Nan replied. 'And she's breathing quite heavily, Ian. I hope she's all right.'

I immediately went through to the dining room, to find Cindy lying in her bed, panting furiously with her tongue hanging out, and looking decidedly agitated.

'What's wrong, lass?' I asked as I knelt down beside her bed. Her tail gave a couple of rather feeble little flicks.

It was her eyes that told me something was not quite right. I stroked her head and she licked the back of my hand a bit anxiously. After a few moments of reassurance, she struggled to her feet, shook her body gingerly and flapped her ears as she always tended to do when emerging from a nap.

'Do you want a wee drink, lass?' I asked, emptying the water out of her bowl before replenishing it with a cool, fresh supply from the kitchen tap. Cindy began shuffling her way into the kitchen.

It was Jillian who noticed it first. 'Dad, Cindy's bleeding,' she remarked innocently.

I looked down, and saw a few spots of bright-red blood dripping from her back end. I then retraced Cindy's steps and the trail splattered all the way back to her bed, which by that time I had noticed was quite wet to the touch. Cindy slumped down on the kitchen floor, and began licking at her rear quarters.

'Good God,' I said to Nan, 'there's something badly wrong here. Can you phone the vet, and I'll see to Cindy?' And in a display of completely uncharacteristic obedience, Nan immediately complied with my suggestion.

Half an hour later, Cindy and I were in the car outside the local veterinary clinic, waiting for Robbie to arrive, as arranged on the telephone. Another ten minutes later, and he was confirming his earlier suspicion that Cindy had contracted Pyometra, a condition that can sometimes affect certain bitches in later adult lift. Pyometra is a potentially nasty infection that almost always requires an immediate hysterectomy, and in those days this was by no means a straightforward operation. She would be under the knife within the hour, Robbie informed me to my great concern.

'Can I spend a few minutes with Cindy?' I asked him.

'Of course you can,' he replied very caringly, if somewhat amused by my insistence on giving my canine charge some human words of encouragement. Robbie then headed off into the surgery's operating theatre where he was joined by his female colleague, a young aspiring student whose name I have completely forgotten through the mists of time. Meanwhile, I sat in the waiting room with Cindy welded to my side and shaking like one of the autumn leaves that, only a few months ago, she would have been chasing up and down the length of Woodroad Park.

'Ready whenever you are, Cindy!' Robbie shouted from behind the sinister big double door of the theatre.

'Cindy, you're going to need a wee operation, lass,' I said to her, looking directly into her eyes.

Her mouth seemed to fall open in horror, and her panting increased still further in rapidity. Her pupils dilated to almost full size, and her whole frame began trembling against my legs.

She was absolutely terrified, no doubt about it. I was too, to be perfectly truthful, and while I did my best to hide the fact, she just knew that her erstwhile master was as scared shitless as she was.

'I want to go home,' her eyes told me. 'And right now!' She got to her feet rather unsteadily, then collapsed back down again in agitated confusion.

'I know you do, Cindy,' I replied, 'but if I take you home now, you won't get any better.'

'I will, if you just take me home. I promise,' her big worried eyes pleaded.

'Cindy, if you don't have this little operation, I might lose you,' I blabbered. 'And how would I ever manage without you? You have to get this done.'

Her entire frame was shaking uncontrollably by this time, no doubt further catalysed by my laughably cumbersome attempts to reassure her.

'Okay, then,' she said, convincing neither herself nor myself. 'But you must promise to give me my favourite treat when I get better and come home.'

'I promise, Cindy,' I replied, stroking her ears gently, but nervously. 'As soon as I leave here, I'll go and get you half-a-dozen tins of oxtail soup.'

She did her best to make her big eyes smile, but it didn't really work. I tried to reciprocate, but to equally miserable effect. Neither of us was fooling the other, and neither of us was in any frame of mind to be fooled. I kissed her on the nose, and she responded by licking my cheek.

'Right Ian, come on!' announced Robbie, as he swung open the operating theatre door. 'Let's get this show on the road!'

'Take good care of her, Robbie,' I said, my lips quivering like a five-year-old on his first day at school. 'She's my best friend.'

'Of course I will,' he replied with a big, confident grin. 'She'll be sitting at the dinner table tomorrow night, and giving you paws for scraps as usual. Right, Cindy, come on and we'll get you sorted!'

And off she went into the theatre, her big bushy tail stuck with congealed blood to the undercarriage that was about to be slit open by Robbie's razor-sharp surgical scalpel. I shuddered at the very thought, turned on my heels and marched out the door of the clinic in the direction of the local supermarket. Try as I might, I just couldn't hold back the tears. I said a little silent prayer to the only one who really understands the universality of every verbal and non-verbal language ever developed by *Homo Sapien, Canis Familiaris* and, no doubt, even a heavenly scattering of hideous extra-terrestrials into the bargain.

'Just let me have my wee dog back. Please, God.'

The deal was that Robbie would phone me in a couple of hours' time, when Cindy was through her operation. She would have to remain in the clinic for at least twenty-four hours, and probably more. When I got home, I explained all of this to Nan and the children, and we attempted to get on with things as usual. Half a dozen half-eaten French fries later, and we realised it just wasn't working. I fidgeted and fretted for another hour or so, and then phoned the clinic. The receptionist informed me that Robbie was out on an emergency call, and put me through to his younger assistant.

'Hello Mr McMurdo,' she said cheerily. 'Cindy has come through her operation well, and is just sleeping off the anaesthetic. She looks quite comfortable.'

I heaved a heavy sigh of relief, and turned to give Nan and the kids the thumbs-up. I could immediately see the tension waning from their worried faces, particularly Nan's.

'When will I be able to take her home? I enquired politely, if a tad impatiently.

'If you come down tomorrow after our morning appointments, we'll have another look at her and see if she is ready to go,' she replied. 'Say about nine-thirty?'

We put Jillian and Derek to bed and sat down to a strong nightcap before retiring wearily, but contentedly, to our own. The thought of Cindy lying in the vet's surgery haunted me all through the night.

I was in the waiting room by nine-fifteen the following morning.

'You're early as usual!' exclaimed Robbie, as he emerged from his consultation with a worried cat owner, to summon in his next patient, a sick cockatoo which lay on the bottom of a cage being carried by an owner who was doubtless as fearful as I had been the previous evening.

'For goodness sake go and get yourself a coffee, or a newspaper, or something that will keep you occupied, and I'll see you in about half an hour,' he teased me with a big warm grin. 'Cindy's fine, Ian!'

I felt rather silly, and immediately did as I was told. However, as I made my way to the door with the words, 'your wish is my command, Robbie,' I soon realised my big mistake. Cindy had just heard my voice. She immediately started barking, and within seconds it was apparent that she had no intention of stopping. Robbie threw his hands in the air.

'Good grief, Amy, go and take Ian through to see Cindy now, or we'll be getting a visit from the Noise Abatement Society. I'll be through in a minute.'

By nine-thirty-five, Cindy was back home to a succession of big hugs and kisses from the whole family, that day thankfully being a Saturday when everyone was at home. Her post-anaesthetic eyes still drooped in exhaustion as she shuffled around rather carefully, but the main thing was that she was home and hosed. Robbie had given me a short list of 'do's and don'ts' about post-operative care, so I reminded everyone that Cindy had just been through a major operation, and a particularly taxing one for a dog of her advancing years, so we all had to be very gentle with her.

Everything went according to plan for the first couple of hours or so, and we just let Cindy sleep it all off in her cosy bed in the dining room. Then, round about lunchtime, I went through to the kitchen and began to make myself a sandwich. At the smell of cold roast chicken, Cindy's nostrils began twitching gently, which encouraged me greatly.

'I know I'm not supposed to give you this, Cindy, but you haven't had anything to eat for almost two days, you poor soul,' I said quietly to her, and she began to rise a bit unsteadily to her feet as I held out the tiniest piece of chicken.

I froze in horror. As she stood there, huge drops of bright red blood drip-drip-dripped from her tummy area onto her now-sodden bed blanket. Her whole undercarriage was saturated in her own blood. Quite how long she had been lying like that was anybody's guess. Two things were certain, though. Firstly, I ought to have been much more vigilant, as she lay recuperating in another room from the one in which I had parked myself in order to give her a bit of peace and quiet. Secondly, Cindy needed emergency treatment. And right now.

'I'm really not feeling well at all,' her big soulful eyes said to me, as I looked at her soaking –wet body.

'I know you're not, lass,' I replied a bit shakily, 'but we're going to make you better.' Neither of us was in the slightest bit convinced.

This time, it was Robbie himself who came to the house to drive Cindy personally down to his surgery. This time, his demeanour was considerably more serious, particularly when he informed us that he feared that Cindy had suffered some kind of organ-related rupture which had caused a massive internal bleed. This time, she was back on the operating table within minutes. And this time, Robbie and three of his assistants were on hand, and the prognosis was not good. My heart sank when he told me that she only had a fifty-fifty chance of making it.

The next few hours were simply dreadful. We all tried to conduct ourselves as normally as possible and, for the sake of the children, Nan and I attempted to be as chirpy and upbeat as we could. However, every time we did so, the huge black cloud that was the horrific spectre of Cindy's imminent demise, descended to remind us of the fact that our desperate fears could well turn into tragic reality.

I must have trudged at least ten anxious miles along our assorted carpets, and gazed at my watch over a hundred times.

It will be at least three hours before we would know anything, Robbie had informed us. Why don't you just take the children down to the park for an hour or so, Nan had suggested to me. Simply because I wanted to hear the news, good or bad, the very second it broke, I had replied more snappily to her than she really deserved.

Half-eleven became noon, noon became one o'clock and, about six hours later, one became two-thirty. At two-thirty-five precisely, the phone rang. I ran and picked it up. It was some guy from a Ford marketing agency, who asked if I'd be interested in purchasing a brand new Sierra for fifteen percent off the on-the-road price. I asked him if he'd be interested in having my right boot surgically removed from his rectum, and slammed the phone down. The second I did so, the bloody thing rang again. Nan and I both jumped.

'Hello,' I said very tentatively.

'Hi Ian, Robbie here,' came the soft-spoken reply. My heart sank at the uncharacteristically solemn tone in his voice.

He went on. 'Ian, Cindy has been through her operation. It took us a long time, but with a great deal of difficulty we eventually located the source of the bleeding and repaired it. What you must understand is that, within the last few days, she has had a hysterectomy followed by a second major operation to repair a serious bleed. She has also had two general anaesthetics within the same timescale. She has lost an awful lot of blood, much of which was, as you know, on your kitchen floor, and she is now on a drip.'

'Will she make it, Robbie?' I asked immediately.

'Too early to tell, Ian. Cindy is a very sick dog, and her body has suffered major trauma. We've sewn her up, she's now heavily sedated and in a very deep sleep. We're trying to get some blood and other essential fluids back into her system, and we really have done all we can for her at this stage.'

'When will we know?' I asked clinically, by this time on emotional autopilot.

'Well, we're hoping she wakes up in about a couple of hours, and we'll assess things from there and let you know.'

'Okay Robbie, the truth please. Is she going to make it or not?'

'I honestly don't know, Ian. What I will say, though, is that it might all come down to one thing.'

'And what's that?'

'Her fighting spirit. Does she really want to fight her way through this, and get home again?'

'Yes she does Robbie, yes she most certainly does.'

'Then she'll make it, Ian.'

'Thanks, Robbie,' I said shakily, but very gratefully for the faint ray of hope he had just given me.

'If I haven't phoned you by four o'clock, you phone me. Okay?'

'Okay. And thanks, Robbie.'

'Don't thank me yet, Ian,' he signed off, and down went the receiver.

If the previous few hours were anxiety-laden, then the next few were even worse. I lost count of the inane conversations that took place that afternoon, and indeed of the silent prayers I offered skywards. Nan and I agreed that there was nothing more we could usefully do anyway and that we would simply have to be patient, not a particularly notable quality of mine, as a good number of family, friends and colleagues would no doubt readily testify.

What we didn't realise was that we would have to wait until nearly six o'clock that evening to receive the welcome news that Cindy had regained consciousness. However, we had not to get our hopes up, because she was still very ill indeed and showing almost no interest in the proceedings. Indeed, the veterinary nurses were finding it impossible to get her to respond to their gentle words of encouragement, let alone persuade her to take even one sip of water. Robbie was still terribly worried about Cindy's condition and, in particular, about her psychological will to survive the trauma of the past two days' terribly invasive procedures.

About eight-thirty that Saturday evening, he phoned me again and told me bluntly that if we couldn't get Cindy to perk up and begin to show some interest in her own recovery, we were going to lose her.

'Ian, in most situations, I would never suggest this at such an early stage after a major operation. However, I really think we need to get Cindy back home with you and the family. It's her only chance. She must start to fight this now, or it's over.'

'Okay, I'll be down immediately,' I replied. 'How do we do this, then?'

'You come down to the surgery with your own car, and we'll lift her gently into the back seat, and then into the house where we can put her in her own bed. I'm hoping that the sounds and scents of what she knows and the people she loves will be enough to rekindle her interest. Ian, she needs her family. It's her only chance.'

The moment Cindy heard my voice in the surgery, her little tail began wagging, albeit rather feebly, and she started crying. The sight of her lying prostrate in a cage, covered in a blanket and with a drip in her thigh, was heartbreaking to behold.

'Just keep talking to her constantly,' Robbie counselled me. 'And get Nan and the kids to do likewise. You must get her interest back. She has to demonstrate a real will to fight this thing, and a real desire to live.'

Half an hour later, and after having negotiated a very tricky procedure, Cindy was lying flat-out in her own cosy bed in the dining room, with everyone blabbering away constantly to her, like sparrows chattering on the swaying branches of an orchard's early summer. Every now and again, she would give a pathetic whimper, and we would take turns to stroke her forehead. After about an hour or so, the successive whimpers became slightly less painful in tone, and her tail began to give a few flicks as we took turns to reassure her. At least she knew she was home, and that was a start.

Cindy had a very, very uncomfortable night, and although she remained fairly motionless in her bed, she really didn't sleep a wink. Nor did Nan or I for that matter, having moved ourselves through to the spare room along with Cindy, in order that we could operate as nursemaids. Nor indeed could Cindy even get up to do the toilet when required, and any liquid or solid effluent had simply to be cleaned up and disposed of, each episode being followed by a deeply apologetic canine whimper and a lovingly reassuring human stroke of the forehead.

Then, quite out of the blue at about five o'clock in the morning, she decided to stretch her head over the rim of her bed in the direction of her water dish. I immediately clambered off my makeshift bed, and pushed the dish over towards her. The sight and sound of Cindy gently lapping the water were all the encouragement that Nan and I could have wished for.

At about seven o'clock and just as daylight was breaking, Jillian and Derek tiptoed gently into our bedroom, to witness the glorious sight of Cindy lying on the floor by my side. As she spied them, her tail gave a couple of wags and she began to stand up rather cautiously. The children laughed and ran over to caress her.

'It's okay, she's been up with me for the past hour now,' I said cheerily, if a bit wearily too. 'And she's even been outside to do her "business", haven't you Cindy?'

The sheer relief on everyone's faces was palpable.

'Cindy was reminding me of something very important,' I announced to the assembled gathering.

'What was that, then?' came the synchronised quizzical reply.

'Two days ago, I promised her that if she was brave enough to go through such a big operation, she would get her favourite treat in all the world. And she hasn't eaten a thing for ages now.'

Jillian's big blue eyes lit up immediately, and she bolted into the kitchen.

'Come on, Cindy,' she shouted excitedly, and the now-recuperating patient began to make her way rather gingerly towards her dinner dish. Her tail wagged gently over the still blood-spattered hind quarters of her feeble body.

'It's your favourite, Cindy! Oxtail soup!' Jillian announced with glee, as she cradled Cindy's weary big head in her arms.

And a few moments later, Nan and I found ourselves beholding the wonderful sight of both our children sitting on the kitchen floor, spoon-feeding the ten-quid puppy with one of Heinz's famous '57 varieties'. On this occasion, the selected variety was the Elixir of Life.

Cindy was back, and I thanked the good lord quietly, but very sincerely.

One Adventure Too Far

'I've got a great ambition to die of exhaustion, rather than boredom'
(Thomas Carlyle, Scottish historian and essayist)

It was a Saturday morning in October, 1987.

As Jillian and Derek pranced expectantly at the front door, all trussed up like Christmas turkeys to protect themselves against the strangely chilly autumnal winds, I laced up my walking boots, aware of the depressing fact that while we were all now kitted out for a Himalayan hike, Cindy would be doing very well just to get to the local park and back. In two months' time, she would be fifteen years of age, God willing. I slipped the lead over her glorious head, and kissed her on the bridge of her nose.

'Once more into the breach!' I announced cheerily, displaying much more raw bravado than genuine optimism.

However, in silent meditation, I actually found myself wondering how many more Saturday morning walks the four musketeers would be able to enjoy together. As my mood began to deepen, I then reminded myself of just how very fortunate we had all been, to have enjoyed so many happy human-canine frolics in the woods over the years, while my poor wife Nan had been able to participate in not a single one. That was the proverbial kick up the arse I had needed, and we all set off cheerfully along the front garden path towards Cumnock's beloved Woodroad Park.

Jillian led the way as usual, with Derek reluctantly having his hand grasped by his over-anxious father, lest he take leave of his senses and bolt across the busy Barrhill Road in front of a twenty-ton articulated lorry. Meanwhile, Cindy plodded along slowly by my side, her tail wagging gently in quiet anticipation of the welcome freedom she would be granted on her imminent, if temporary release into the joys of the autumn foliage. What none of us realised at that moment was that this would be our very last walk together.

As soon as we had left the final traffic-bearing tarmac surface of Bank Avenue, I let Cindy off her lead, and the exuberant if mildly pissed-off Derek was similarly set free from my vice-like clutches. All four of us then set off down the sloping path that would take us to the steep banks of the River Lugar, where we would perform the customary ritual of throwing a few sticks into the big pool for Cindy to swim after and fetch. Like most Labrador Retrievers, she had always loved the water and would happily have swam and paddled for hours on end. However, very strangely on this occasion, she was for none of it.

'Daddy, why is Cindy not chasing my stick?' Jillian enquired a bit anxiously.

'I don't know, lass,' I replied. 'Perhaps she's not feeling too well, or maybe she's just a wee bit tired.'

Both Jillian and Derek immediately clocked that my response to such a simple question was unconvincing in the extreme.

'How can Cindy be tired when she's been sleeping all night, Daddy?' asked Derek.

'Yes, that's right, Daddy,' opined Jillian, 'she slept all night, and all morning after her breakfast, so it's silly to say that she's tired.'

They refused to let go.

'Well, maybe she's sick,' I replied, rolling my eyes towards the heavens. Here we bloody go again, another in-depth cross-examination, another relentless interrogation. If these two ever become procurators fiscal, God help the accused, I thought to myself.

'But she's not sick either, Daddy,' continued Derek, 'because if she was sick, there would be sickness all over the road, and all over your shoes, and all over the carpet. Big blobs of yellow slimy, smelly sickness. And there would be ………'

'RIGHT! I get the picture!' I retorted, realising that this

increasingly graphic conversation had the potential to last well into the afternoon. So I continued with my frantic attempts to put a lid on it.

'Okay, maybe she's just not feeling very well, and doesn't want to play. Simple as that,' I continued, more in hope than expectation of their eventual acceptance of my hastily-devised hypothesis.

The sight of Cindy trudging wearily along the grassy riverbank did worry me, though. It was most unusual, since given any opportunity whatsoever, she would normally have dived headlong into the river without a single moment's hesitation. That day, though, she simply wasn't interested. Something was up. I knew it and the kids knew it.

'Come on then,' I said, and we all climbed up the banking and walked back down the half-dozen steps onto the footbridge which provided the only means of crossing the river without getting one's feet wet. Once we had negotiated the flat surface of the bridge, Cindy suddenly stopped in her tracks, stared in awe at the next ten steps that would take us up and into Woodroad Park, and slumped down at my feet.

'What's wrong, lass?' I asked her anxiously, as she lay there panting. Her eyes told me the whole story. She was simply exhausted.

I did my best to reassure the kids, then realised that I had a decision to make. As luck would have it, we had reached the furthest-away point of our circular route, and there were now two clear choices. Should we turn around and go back again, which would mean climbing back up the steep path before we reached the main road, or should we push on, get Cindy up the steps somehow and then onto the flat grassy area of the park, which could be accessed by car if it were to prove necessary? I decided on the latter course of action.

We let Cindy rest for a few minutes and, thankfully, her panting eventually receded somewhat, although her breathing remained a good deal faster than normal. The children managed to coax her back onto her feet, and the sight of her tail beginning to wag again was indeed one for sore eyes. With a bit of encouragement and cajoling from all three of us, she managed to pull herself up the first four steps unaided. However, she then sat back down again, and the heavy panting returned, at which point I decided that enough was enough. I slipped my arms underneath her torso and physically lifted her up the remaining steps to the meadow, then placed her down on the grass.

'Let's just sit with Cindy for a wee while,' I said to Jillian and Derek, and they nodded in uncharacteristically silent acquiescence.

So for the next few minutes we just sat there, stroking Cindy's head and talking to her reassuringly. All three of us were clearly very worried about what had just happened and why it had happened, although not one of us verbalised our fears. Some ten minutes or so later, we had again coaxed Cindy back onto her feet and we set off in the direction of our home, which was still about half a mile away.

'If we take things slowly, Cindy will get her strength back and she'll be fine,' I informed my offspring, realising that it was in nobody's interests – and certainly not in Cindy's – for tension or especially panic to be allowed to enter the equation.

After another few minutes, during which we must only have covered a maximum of around one hundred metres, we had almost reached the front door of the large imposing building that famously housed one of Ayrshire's – and Scotland's – last remaining outdoor swimming pools. By this time, I had concluded that, if it became absolutely necessary, I could collect my car and drive it all the way along the single-track road and over the grass, right to Cindy's side. However, she was doing just fine and in all probability we would manage to humour her into plodding her weary way home, if only at a snail's pace. However, by that stage, I had recognised that this would be Cindy's swansong, at least as far as semi-adventurous walks were concerned.

No sooner had I entertained that very depressing thought, than Cindy collapsed in a heap at my feet.

'DADDY!' screamed Jillian.

'WHAT'S WRONG WITH CINDY?' yelled Derek.

As my poor, exhausted Cindy lay prostrate on the grass of her favourite park, panting furiously and with her eyes rolling around in their sockets, both Jillian and Derek started sobbing. I looked around, and to my consternation, realised that there was not a soul in sight. The swimming pool was closed for the season, and even its shop windows had been shuttered up to deter would-be vandals. Likewise, the entrance to the adjacent putting green was adorned by a 'Closed For The Season' notice, with an identical one nailed onto the attendant's hut which, had this tragic event happened in the summer months, would have provided me with someone to offer moral support and practical assistance.

So there we all were, a despairing father-and-master, two young children beside themselves with anxiety, a very sick and elderly dog, and all of us still awaiting the invention some ten years later of the mobile phone. We were in a really tricky predicament, and we all knew it. The most important thing, I persuaded the kids, was for everyone to stay really, really calm, because if we became upset, then Cindy would get upset too. They took very little convincing.

As we sat on the grass stroking Cindy's head, which by this time was resting on my lap, I had to think very quickly. There were several options open to me, but not one of them was particularly appealing. I could send the children off to ring someone's front door bell and ask the resident good Samaritan to call the vet to come to Cindy's rescue, while I looked after her, but the nearest house was a good distance away. I could ask Jillian and Derek to stay with Cindy while I ran to the vet's house, but it was even further away. There again, I could run home, explain the situation to Nan, and ask her to contact the vet while I grabbed the car keys and drove back to collect Cindy and the kids.

Recognising that not one of the aforementioned options was in any way attractive, I chose the third. I told both Jillian and

Derek that they must stay very, very calm, that they must not under any circumstances go off anywhere with a stranger, no matter what he or she might offer to do to help Cindy, and promised them that I would be back within fifteen minutes. I was there in ten, principally on account of the fact that I was an extremely fit young man in these days, my suppleness the result of a pretty energetic training regime, but no doubt augmented that morning by the waves of adrenalin coursing through my veins.

A few minutes later, Jillian and Derek were back home telling the tale to their mum, and Cindy was lying on the vet's examination table. After a thorough clinical examination, followed by administration of various intravenous medicines, Robbie ushered me back into the examination room and gave me the bad news.

'Cindy's had a heart attack, Ian,' he said solemnly. 'Thankfully, it's been a fairly mild one, but it has really knocked her for six. I've given her some medication and, with a bit of rest, she should recover reasonably well.'

'What's the prognosis, Robbie? Straight up, no bullshit,' I enquired, exhibiting much more outward courage than I felt in my stomach.

'She's an old dog, Ian, and she's had a great life. She's almost fifteen years old now, and while she's not quite past her sell-by date, she's now living on borrowed time. If you look after her, she'll see her next birthday, but she won't see the one after that. I'm sorry, Ian, but that's a dog's life for you.'

'Okay. Can I take her home?' I asked, choking back the tears to protect my dignity. 'I want her to spend all the time she has left with the family.'

'Of course you can,' he replied, and added with a smile, 'she's a hardy old soul, you know!'

I thanked Robbie, stuffed God-knows how many packets of canine prescription medicines into the hip pockets of my denims, and carried Cindy out to the car where I lay her down on the back seat. Five minutes later, she was again stretched out contentedly in her own cosy bed, with the love of her family providing all the warmth and comfort she would ever need again.

That evening was undoubtedly one of *déjà vu*, as I again found myself sitting on my favourite chair in the living room, with yet more research literature in one hand and a generous glass of whisky in the other. I was utterly determined that Cindy's remaining days with us would be as comfortable and happy as possible, and so I realised that I simply had to develop a really good understanding of the physiology and psychology of canine ill-health. Put another way, I needed to know a bit more about how Cindy was feeling emotionally, before attempting to have what I just instinctively knew would be a very important and unavoidably difficult 'discussion' with her. Robbie had assured me that as a consequence of the drugs he had administered, Cindy would sleep like a puppy for at least two hours. So I got to work, aided and abetted by three fingers of the *Bold John Barleycorn*.

What I discovered was really quite fascinating and, yet again, served to illustrate just how much more adept dogs are in certain situations than their human counterparts, especially in terms of adapting to adversity. You see, when a dog displays the usual symptoms of illness, such as unresponsiveness, lethargy and loss of appetite, we simply conclude that these symptoms are the direct consequence of its illness. However, nine times out of ten, we would be well off the mark.

The fact is that, whereas you and I might crave a bit of mollycoddling when we are feeling a bit under the weather, the dog behaves quite differently. Indeed, its apathy, enforced starvation and leave-me-alone demeanour are, more often than not, its very first line of defence against the illness itself. All the poor thing is actually trying to do is get some peace and quiet, and for very good reason too. The dog is simply trying to buy itself some recuperation time, in order to let its own immune system kick in. No need for a bowl of chicken soup, a savoury biscuit or even a little cuddle. It is simply depriving itself of food to ensure that nature's nasty little disease-causing microbes are starved of fuel, thus preventing them from doing even more damage, and of quite unnecessary and unwanted attention in order to get enough rest to build up its strength again. Perhaps that's another little lesson we should try to learn from our more clued-in canine friends.

However, what I found really remarkable was that dogs have very little fear of death, indeed perhaps even none. Whether they fully appreciate the sheer enormity of the chasm between their own mortality and their inevitable demise is something you and I might never know, but for some strange reason they just don't fear it.

If you ask your own vet, he or she will tell you that, alas, very few dogs actually die 'naturally' these days. The vast majority die either from fatal accidents or are humanely 'put to sleep' as a result of chronic illness, the latter of course being a privilege that is currently unavailable to human beings in this country of ours, no matter the level of suffering involved. However, if you ask the owners of dogs who have actually died of natural causes, they will invariably tell you that the poor things just sought peace in the end, by wandering away into another room or into the far corner of the vegetable patch, simply to allow themselves the privacy to slip away with dignity.

In Cindy's case there were, of course, no nasty microbes involved. She had suffered a heart attack, plain and simple. However, she was very ill, and I was now suitably enlightened by my latest piece of clumsy-but-necessary research. And while I would never really know exactly what was going through Cindy's mind as she lay there recuperating, I had learned one very important thing. As she prepared for the inevitability of the lowering of her final curtain, she had absolutely no fear of it.

On the other hand and as a mere *Homo Sapien*, I simply dreaded the day that Cindy would ultimately be taken away from me. The ten-quid puppy had been my heart, my soul, my conscience, my everything. And there was one other thing I knew for certain.

That day was just around the corner.

Losing My Soul

'Death leaves a heartache no one can heal,
love leaves a memory no one can steal.'
(Inscription on an Irish headstone)

Ever since Cindy's double operation, and most certainly since that red letter day in Woodroad Park almost one year previously, I always knew on an intellectual level at least that Cindy really was living on borrowed time. Psychologically, however, I never could admit that dark contemplation to myself or share it with Nan, not even in my most vulnerable and self-pitying moments. And, trust me, there were a few.

It's a strange thing, a loved one's impending demise, but for the first time in our lives together, a strange sort of incompatibility gradually began to develop in the relationship between Cindy and me. Put another way, I found myself wishing to spend as much time as possible sitting by her side and just talking to her, while she clearly just wanted to be left alone, to sleep and dream about the wonderful life she had lived. Into the bargain, and unlike hopelessly fret-filled human beings, she had no fear of stepping through the great door of uncertainty that all of us will surely have to contemplate at some stage.

The change in the family's routine was considerable, as was the effect on my own lifestyle in particular. No longer did the alarm clock ring at seven o'clock on a Saturday morning, in order to remind the head of the household to get three of the four most important 'people' in his life fed, watered and kitted out for the weekly adventures up and down the Muirkirk hills, or around the mighty Afton reservoir. No longer did Nan need to hide giggling under the bedclothes every weekday in life, to avoid herself being scratched and licked half to death by a hyperactive mutt. And no longer did I need to change from my dark pin-striped suit, white shirt and outrageously luminescent tie into my walking gear when I returned home from work at the end of yet another day's toils. No, I'm afraid that all Cindy wanted to do by that time was to eat, drink and doze away her well-earned retirement days.

And, boy, how I missed the old routine. Very soon, I managed to put on an impressive amount of weight, and even more significantly, I lost a great deal of the *joie de vivre* that had previously characterised my whole approach to life, some of which had frequently reached the point of driving others round the bloody bend with my quite infamous levels of energy and gusto.

'For God's sake, buy a mountain bike or something,' Nan said one evening in pure exasperation, at yet again finding me lying slouched on the settee with a cup of coffee and a Jammy Dodger biscuit, when hitherto I would have been out of the house with Cindy, and out of her hair while she was making the dinner.

'Just do something, Ian' she nagged. 'Anything at all!'

A couple of years back, Nan and I had joined the local bowling club, the sport itself having proved to be the perfect antidote for my gradually escalating professional responsibilities, but the recreational side of which, paradoxically, had only served to increase my own consumption of fine ales by a factor of 'X' (where 'X' is a whole number between 9 and 11).

I actually enjoyed bowling very much indeed at the time, but the associated new and much more slovenly recreational lifestyle was by then at least two quantum levels below my earlier fitness regime, that had very religiously consisted of twenty-five press-ups and twenty-five sit-ups every single morning in life, together with at least twenty-five miles per week tramping the hills with Cindy. Sadly, I had now allowed these to be replaced by a roughly similar number of pints of lager, and frequent rides home in smoke-filled taxis on account of the sheer effort involved in walking the three-quarters-of-a-mile back to my house.

One day, after having been persuaded by a rather enterprising insurance salesman to apply for yet another life cover policy, I was called in for a medical examination in nearby Ayr. The medical itself went fine, and the doctor gave me a copy of his findings in a brown envelope. However, my eyeballs fell out of their sockets when I opened the envelope in the car, only to find that I had assaulted the scales at fourteen-stones-and-ten pounds, some two stones heavier than I had been only a couple of years back. I went home, looked at my big red face in the bathroom mirror, and felt physically sick. The shocked reflection looked as if someone had blown up my big coupon with a bicycle pump. My self-esteem immediately dived in the direction of my boots, where I knew it would remain until I got up off my big fat arse and did something about it.

One Sunday morning in early October, I found myself sitting on the living room floor beside Cindy. I rolled her over on her back as usual, and began rubbing her belly. Her tail wag-wag-wagged as always, and when I stopped, she pawed at me for more.

'You might not have the same 'oomph' you once had, Cindy,' I said to her, 'but you're still full of beans, old girl!' She pawed at my arm once more.

'I've got more 'oomph' than you've got!' her still-bright eyes replied, to my complete surprise.

'What?' I asked, slightly puzzled.

'Look at you now,' she replied. 'You look like Humpty Dumpty!'

'Where did that come from, Cindy?' I asked, a bit put out. 'Come on, if you've got something to say, bloody say it,' I invited her, if somewhat less than wholeheartedly.

'Ian, if I was as fit today as I was only a couple of years ago, you wouldn't be able to keep up with me now,' she opined. 'I'd have to leave you in the car, and collect you once I had come back from the woods.'

'As bad as that, do you think?' I enquired, very tentatively.

'Worse,' she replied. 'A lot worse. You need to get your act together. For Nan, for the children, and for yourself.'

'But I miss our big walks, Cindy,' I said without all that much conviction.

'Don't use me as an excuse!' she retorted indignantly. 'You need to get up off your backside and start exercising again. And you need to stop going out to that bowling green every second night. I've lost count of the number of times you come back reeking of beer, and then slump into your big chair in front of the television with a plate of food that would feed a whole army. You need to get back to being as fit and healthy as you used to be.'

'But I can't, Cindy,' I said pathetically, 'because things aren't the way they used to be, are they?'

'No, and they never can be,' she replied. 'But they could be really good again for you and your family.'

'I really miss the good old days, Cindy,' I said ruefully.

'I know you do, but these days will always be in your dreams, and they'll always be in mine,' she said calmly, but very surefootedly, eyeballing me with one of her near-hypnotic gazes. 'But you must move ahead with your life, Ian. You must get fit again, and get the zest back into your life, and start living again. Promise me.'

'I just can't stand the thought of losing you, Cindy,' I blurted out. 'I just can't.'

'You will never lose me, Ian,' her big honest face replied with deep, deep sincerity. 'And that's a promise. I'll always be watching over you. And over Nan and the kids.'

I began to sob uncontrollably, as I cradled her big beautiful forehead in my arms.

'Come on, it's your turn now,' her bright eyes proclaimed, looking at me with devastating reassurance. 'Promise me that you'll move on with your life.'

Words wouldn't come.

'PROMISE ME!' her eyes screamed at me. I nearly jumped out of my skin.

'I promise, Cindy!' I conceded immediately.

'And you'll get another dog.?' she added. 'Okay?'

'Oh, come on, Cindy, how can I ....?'

'PROMISE ME!'

'Okay, ... I, ... I promise,' I relented. 'But only when I feel I'm ready. Okay?'

'Okay!' Cindy responded rather more acceptingly, before adding, 'now if it's all the same to you, I'm bushed and I'd like a nap before my dinner.'

I kissed her mighty forehead and left her in peace. That night, I slept like a new-born baby for the first time in ages. Somehow, I just knew where my life was going again.

A cold, damp and decidedly gloomy Monday morning defined the archetypal, miserable late-autumn climate that we in the west of Scotland have come to love and cherish. No wonder the Scottish suicide rate is at its worst at this time of the bloody year, I muttered to myself, as I closed the big oak door behind me to begin my twenty-seven mile journey to school, where a few adolescent miscreants would doubtless be lining up outside my office door in an hour or two, to receive their customised words of wisdom from yours truly. Great kids they all were, really, but some of them were facing a range of daily challenges from which many of us have been sheltered all through our fortunate and over-protected lives. I simply adored my job.

One of my many duties, in the multi-faceted role of Assistant Head, was that of chairing a fundraising committee. We met every fourth Monday at four o'clock, which meant that I wouldn't get home until well after seven on those particular days. Our early October meeting had proved to be very productive and uplifting, as evidenced by the exceedingly healthy sum of money we had raised from a recent sponsored walk involving the whole school population, and by the sight of us all standing in the rain-soaked car park, congratulating each other on our respective performances. I vividly remember everyone laughing and joking in the rain, our collective mood in stark contrast to the gathering gloom of the evening. Little did I realise that this would be the last time I would laugh for quite a while.

When I returned home shortly after seven, Nan had the dinner all ready and waiting, God bless her. Scotch broth soup it was, followed by a hearty main course of beef stew, mashed potatoes and boiled cabbage, just perfect for a decidedly miserable October evening. My stomach rumbled in anticipation, as I marched up the stairs to replace the obligatory suit-shirt-and-tie uniform with the more optional denims-T-shirt-and-trainers alternative in which I always felt much, much more comfortable.

'Do you want your dinner, lass?' I asked Cindy, as she shuffled slowly into the kitchen, sniff-sniff-sniffing the wonderfully appetising odours that were emanating from the big pots on Nan's stove. The sight of her showing some interest in food was a very welcome one, since she had been demonstrating very little appetite over the past few days, something that I had discussed with our vet only the previous evening.

'She'll eat when she needs to, and when she wants to,' Robbie had replied, supremely matter-of-fact as usual. 'Cindy is very old now, so just let her be, and let her do things at her own pace. And for goodness sake, Ian, stop worrying about her. She's had a terrific innings, and she's still soldiering along nicely.'

I put a couple of spoonfuls of Cindy's regular food in a bowl, and nicked a ladleful of Nan's beef gravy from the pot, then mixed it all in together, before putting her big plastic dinner dish down on the kitchen floor.

'You spoil that dog, Ian, you really do!' Nan remarked with a smile. Tragically, it would be the very last time I would ever get the chance to do just that.

As Cindy began licking rather half-heartedly at her dinner, her legs suddenly gave way, and she crashed onto the floor with an almighty 'THUMP!'

'CINDY!' Nan screamed, as she wheeled herself over to Cindy's side, as fast as her arms could propel her.

'Nan, could you phone Robbie right away?' I said much more calmly than I actually felt. 'I'll see to Cindy.'

I told Derek and Jillian to go upstairs immediately, under the pretext of Cindy needing a little rest, but I'm sure they too realised how very, very serious the situation was. I just didn't want the wee souls to have to witness the inevitable happening in front of their own eyes, God forbid. As Nan made the desperate phone call through in the dining room, I sat beside Cindy's prostrate body on the cold floor.

'Don't you leave me, Cindy!' I said through fast-developing tears, as I slipped a blanket under her head and pulled another one over her panting frame. 'Just think of the battles you've fought. And you've won every one of them, lass. Every single one!'

Cindy's breathing became more and more laboured, and her eyes were becoming increasingly heavy.

'Come on, Cindy,' I sobbed. 'Come on, you're going to get through this, just like the last time. Aren't you, lass? Robbie's on his way up to help you again. NAN, WHERE'S THAT F-----G VET?'

Cindy opened her big brown eyes for what I just instinctively knew would be the very last time. They tried to look at me, but the spark was gone. Gone for ever. I kissed her on the nose, as the tears ran down my cheeks and splattered onto her forehead.

Just at that, and with one last almighty effort, she lifted her right paw from the floor, and plopped it straight into the palm of my own right hand. She had never, ever done anything like that before, not even once in the fifteen years we had lived our lives together.

I grabbed her paw, and immediately realised that she was trying to get my attention. I looked at her tired old face.

'Write it down on pieces of paper, Ian,' her eyes smiled feebly. 'And some day you can share our secret language.'

'I will, Cindy,' I sobbed, 'but not for a long, long time. It has to be our secret for a while yet.'

Then I knew it was time. Time for Cindy's final wordless message.

'Some day soon, I'll meet you at the gate.'

And then her eyes fell closed for the very last time, and her body fell limp in my arms.

Robbie and his young assistant rang the doorbell about one minute later. Robbie examined Cindy briefly, then turned to me and said through moist eyes, 'She's gone, Ian. I'm very, very sorry. She was a wonderful big dog.'

I hugged Cindy tightly in my arms for a minute or so, before kissing her goodbye.

Then she was carried out of the only home she had ever known in a black body bag.

The Return Of The Dogless Child

'Advice is what we ask for when we already know the answer, but wish we didn't.'
(Erica Jong, Novelist and Poet)

I have simply lost count of the number of people who have told me over the years that they would never, ever have a dog in the family, citing as irrefutable evidence the inevitable heartache that must surely befall them some day on account of the pure pragmatics involved, viz., the very fact that life expectancy in the canine species tends to be considerably shorter than that of our own. While they are most certainly correct on the numerical count, what deeply misguided souls they are in a spiritual sense. They just don't know what they have been missing.

The people I feel really sorry for are not those who have already mourned their dog's tragic passing, nor indeed those who have developed some kind of fear or aversion to dogs, however rational or irrational their particular phobias might be. No, my sympathies are with those who would secretly have loved to own a dog, but who have persuaded themselves, or worse still been brainwashed by others, that dog ownership is 'too tying' in a social context, or 'too upsetting' when the grim reaper comes calling (or too something else for that matter). In my view, these poor unfortunate souls have just unwittingly deprived themselves of a lifetime of love and friendship that is simply unique.

Yes it is true that in the most general terms, we might reasonably expect to live some six or seven times as long as most dogs do, even taking on board the quite considerable variation in longevity across the numerous canine breeds. So if you do eventually decide to acquire your own pooch, you'd best be aware that you will almost certainly outlive it, and therefore have to suffer the inevitable heartache of the poor thing's terribly sad demise further down the road. It's always better to go into any new project with one's eyes open, don't you think?

However, even taking into full account the fact that I have now felt three separate daggers through my heart, each agonising stab associated with the tragic passing of one of my wonderful big dogs, I can tell you this. My own life has been made exponentially richer for having lived almost all of it with *Canis Familiaris*. Without a question of a doubt, I would never, ever have wanted it any other way.

Make no mistake, though, dog ownership is a very responsible business. It really saddens me when I watch a television documentary about the daily vanloads of poor, abandoned but otherwise healthy Christmas-present puppies that find their way into such depressing but necessary abodes as Battersea Dogs' Home, most of whom are blissfully unaware of the gruesome death sentence that might very well require to be pronounced upon them any day now. It angers me when I see an emaciated dog roaming about the streets dodging the traffic, as it scampers from dustbin to dustbin in search of any morsels of food that have been discarded from someone else's bulging larder, or nibbles at some drunken moron's regurgitated Saturday night takeway. It appals me every time I see a dog fouling a public park, as the poor thing's alleged master pours a can of beer over his throat whilst watching the youngsters play football around the offending article. And it makes my heart sink every time I read about some poor child who has been mauled by someone's dog, simply because it has never been trained to behave in a socially acceptable way.

Quite simply, if you're not prepared to take responsibility for your dog, and to feed, exercise, train and shower him or her with affection, then you should never, ever be allowed to own one. You may well have your own view about such matters, but that is mine, and I'm afraid you'll just have to like it or lump it.

Anyway, that little self-opinionated health warning aside, I cannot even begin to explain in mere human words the sheer happiness and joy that dog ownership has given my family and myself over the years, nor indeed the social, psychological and emotional richness with which our dogs have blessed us. Together with the family, they have shared every moment of heartache and joy, every episode of failure and success, and every emotion of deep dread and boundless optimism. Quite simply, they have each lived the lives that we ourselves have lived.

Not a single one of my dogs has ever been phased, or even discouraged in the slightest, by the bad news that the postman has just dropped through the letter box, or that the medical staff have relayed over the phone. And each of them, without a single exception, has always behaved like a hyperactive child when some great news has lifted our spirits and allowed us yet again to wallow in our considerable good fortune. Our big dogs have always been there for us during the good times, and unfailingly throughout the bad. Never once did they give a tuppeny damn about the next impending financial dilemma, or the latest depressing medical prognosis. All they ever wanted to do was to be there, right by our sides, converting every jittery moment of embryonic weakness and self-doubt into warm emotions of optimism and lust-for-life. In short, our dogs have been our lives, and we sincerely hope that we have been theirs.

And so it had always been with my late beloved Cindy, who had been welded to Nan's and my own side ever since that wonderful moment over fifteen years previously, when the farmer's wife had proudly slid open the mighty barn door to allow the 'special' one of ten heavenly eight-week-old Andrex puppies to choose to take up lifelong residence in our new home. Make no mistake; it was Cindy who had chosen Nan and me that day, not the other way around.

If the evening of Cindy's tragic passing was difficult, then the following day was at least ten times worse. Nan and I had agreed that we would present ourselves to our children as a veritable example of strong parental leadership and staunch resilience, the very epitome of self-discipline itself, if you will. I remember how easily the words came out at the time, but in the event, just how utterly impossible it then proved to conduct ourselves in the manner we had intended.

We packed the kids off to school as usual, despite their tearful protests, and I set off likewise to my own, leaving Nan all alone with her demons to confront. Having drifted along in some kind of deeply-troubled daze all morning, I eventually nipped off work in the early afternoon, to drive home and give Nan and myself a good hour or so to clear away Cindy's personal belongings, before Jillian and Derek could return to witness such an awful thing. I honestly think that was the worst part of all.

We agreed that everything should simply be chucked into a big plastic bin bag, not unlike the one poor Cindy's limp body had been bundled into less than twenty-four hours previously. So into the bag went her red lead, her brown leather collar, all her squeaky Christmas toys, her two fluffy blankets, her food and water dishes and finally, we thought, her assorted medical supplies.

'You won't be needing these any more, Cindy,' I blurted out as bravely as I could through my very stiff upper lip, as I threw a tube of canine ear drops and an aerosol tin of dog deodorant into the plastic bag.

Nan just sat there beside me in her wheelchair, staring through glassy eyes into the distance. I noticed that she was cradling something in her right hand.

'What's that?' I asked.

She just opened her hand in total silence, revealing the chewed stump of the wire hairbrush that she had used to groom Cindy's coat every single day for the last fifteen years. I felt as if someone had just hit me in the guts with a sledgehammer.

However, it wasn't until I eventually emerged from the house, to throw the bin liner and Cindy's big blue plastic bed into the back seat of the car in preparation for my intended visit to the local landfill site, that the enormity of the situation finally hit me. Because there lying on the floor mat, was the big bag of dog biscuits that went everywhere with us, in order to operate as a reward mechanism for the occasional moment of canine compliance.

'And you won't be needing these either, Cindy,' I said trying to force a little laugh. And it was at that point that my composure collapsed in a heap.

I think it was the sheer suddenness of the transformation from an enforced laugh one moment, into a quite uncontrollable deluge of tears the very next, that really caught me by complete surprise. As I knelt on the back seat of the car, with my legs sticking out sideways and my feet a few centimetres above the wet pavement, I just started sobbing and sobbing like a baby.

Nan, who had been sitting just inside the big front door at the time, witnessing the final exodus of Cindy's few earthly possessions, saw what was happening and immediately wheeled herself out into the rain. She just wrapped her arms around me.

'Come on,' she said, squeezing my hand. Then we went back inside our home to begin the rest of our lives.

Our lives without Cindy.

The minutes went by and turned into hours, the hours to days, and the days to weeks and eventually months. Almost one year after Cindy died, and having acted most obediently on the wise counsel that she herself had earlier given me while we had been sitting cheek-by-jowl on an Ayrshire hillside, I found myself turning the key for the very last time in the big oak door of the only home our family had ever known.

As I joined Nan, Jillian and Derek in the car, *en route* to our new lives in our new custom-built bungalow at the other end of town, there was total silence, save for the swish-swish-swish of the windscreen wipers that might have been more productively deployed on our respective cheeks.

Then one Sunday morning about a month later, having got ourselves reasonably well settled into our new home by that time, the weekly newspapers dropped through our letterbox onto the pristine hall carpet. With Nan still in bed enjoying her much-deserved weekly lie-in, and the kids out playing on last Christmas's bicycles with their recently-acquired new chums, I made myself some coffee and toast, then began thumbing my way through the Sunday papers. After I had leafed through the leading news items, followed by the much more intellectually-demanding sports pages, for some strange reason I found myself wading through the 'classified ads' section, which happened to be set out in four vertical columns.

Having chuckled my arrogant way through the assorted and very confused range of gadgets for sale. including to my huge amusement, a *very attractive and easy-to-clean pigeon-droppings scraper, only £4.50 + VAT + P & P'*, my eyes were somehow drawn to the garden furniture collection, presumably because our new abode was standing on what was still much more of a building site than anything even remotely resembling a garden.

For some strange reason, the one that caught my eye was the following.

'For sale, wooden gates, any size, customised to your own requirements.

We have a very special gate, just for you.

Estimates on request.'

'Gates?' I asked myself, a bit puzzled. "'I'll meet you at the gate!" That was what Cindy said, wasn't it?'

I scratched my chin, and refilled my coffee mug.

'Gate? What bloody gate?' I asked myself again. 'I wonder what she was on about?'

I got up from the kitchen table and wandered into the lounge towards the big stone-built fireplace on the gable wall, immediately above which hung a portrait of my beloved Cindy, which still has pride of place to this very day, I might add. As I stood there with my coffee cup in one hand, I stroked the outline of her jet-black nose with the other, and looked deep into her big intelligent eyes.

'What gate, Cindy?' I asked very quietly. 'What did you mean when you said you would meet me at the gate?'

Cindy just smiled at me through her big brown eyes as always, the only not-too-subtle difference being that they were now encased in a wooden frame behind a slab of non-reflective glass, rather than radiating from the glorious forehead that only a few months back would have responded so affectionately to my caress.

How I missed my big dog.

I trudged melancholically back through to the kitchen, and looked again at the entrepreneurial carpenter's advert. Bloody gates, I muttered to myself.

Just at that, eight-year-old Derek came bursting in through the back door at his customary breakneck speed, immediately followed by two of his new best pals.

'Can we get some sweeties?' he asked. 'Please, Dad?'

'Only if you tell me what you think this advertisement is about,' I teased him.

'Okay!' he shouted. 'Which one?'

Without really looking all that carefully, I just nonchalantly tap-tap-tapped the tip of my ballpoint pen over what I thought was the enterprising gate maker's PR masterpiece.

'Read it out loud,' I said to him, with a cheeky grin.

'And if you read it perfectly – and I mean perfectly - I'll give you and your buddies a tube of Smarties each,' I added naughtily, testing not only his resolve, but also the impressive academic progress that his primary-four teacher had been telling Nan about in the supermarket, just a couple of days earlier.

Derek then sat down at the kitchen table, with his two equally-focused minders at either shoulder, looked at the advert that my pen had been pointing towards, and began reading it out.

Very slowly and very, very deliberately.

'FOR SALE.
SIX GOLDEN RETRIEVER PUPPIES.
SEVEN WEEKS OLD.
READY NOW. '

Open-mouthed, I stared at the classifieds section, and immediately clocked that I had been pointing not at the one purporting to sell bespoke wooden gates, but to one immediately adjacent to it in the next column, listed under 'Pets and Livestock'. A shiver ran up my spine.

'Y-Y-Y-Y-E-S-S-S-S-S!' shouted Derek, clench-fisted and egged on, of course, by his ultra-impressed sidekicks, at which point they all scarpered back out the door at similarly high velocity, clutching their precious sweeties as if their very survival depended on them.

As they ran down the garden path, I overheard Derek adding with scarcely-restrained ecstasy, 'And we're going to get a new pup as well!'

I grimaced, as I thought of the corrective discussion that would require to take place in an hour or so, in order to clear up this terrible misunderstanding.

I then tiptoed back into the lounge, rather uneasily I must say. By this time, the sun's early morning rays were already shining through our massive fourteen-foot-wide picture window, and illuminating the fireside wall. Cindy's portrait seemed to be on fire in the golden beams of sunlight. I looked at her beautiful face again, and noticed that the pink tip of her tongue appeared to be much more prominent than ever in the brilliant sunlight.

'Are you trying to tell me something, lass?' I asked a bit tentatively.

'Might be!' I beseeched her eyes to tease me, as if she had never left my side.

I gazed into her eyes for a good minute or so, more in hope than expectation that I would once more sense the beginning of yet another hypnotic two-way flow of vital information being communicated between us in our very secret *Dogmanese*.

Nothing. Absolutely nothing.

Then rather despondently, I turned to walk away. Just as I began closing the lounge door behind me, I caught the slightest movement in my peripheral vision.

'Did you wink at me there, Cindy?' I asked, and stared at her portrait again. Total silence, both audible and visual. However, there was now something very striking about her face. It was her eyes.

They were absolutely ablaze in the sun's dazzling rays.

I smiled and walked back into the kitchen, by which time my smile had turned to a giggle, then my giggle to a proper belly laugh. I took a big blue *Magic Marker* out of the drawer, and circled the advert that Derek had read out to me only a couple of minutes earlier.

Then I grabbed the telephone.

Heaven's Gate

'*Dogs are our link to paradise. They don't know evil, or jealousy, or discontent. To sit with a dog on a hillside on a glorious afternoon is to be back in Eden, where doing nothing was not boring, it was peace.*'
(Milan Kundera, Czech Author and Poet)

Heaven's Gate is hidden away in a grassy meadow, beside a bubbling stream
It is a happy place, very peaceful and very, very secret
On one side of Heaven's Gate there are houses, cars and lots of bustling noise
On the other there is only peace, and tranquillity

Dogs roam freely in the meadow, where they play together from dusk till dawn
They have plenty of food and they drink from the fresh waters of the stream
They bask in the glorious sunshine and sleep contentedly under the beams of moonlight
Their aches and pains are gone forever

Life is perfect, absolutely perfect, apart from one thing
They have all left behind a loving family, who were very special to them
They miss them so very much that their hearts still pine for them
And they each yearn for their master's strong voice and gentle touch

As they drift asleep under the stars, they remember
the walks through the woods
The fun-filled games with squeaky toys, the trips to
the beach
They can still smell their loved ones' skin and feel
their loving cuddles
And they miss them so very, very badly

Then one morning, as they play in the meadow,
something catches one dog's attention
She stops, tilts her head from side to side and stares
excitedly into the distance
It couldn't be him? Could it? Let it be him, please!
Then the voice she thought she would never hear
again sounds across the stream

'Come on lass, we're going home!'
She runs frantically across the field towards her
beloved master
They roll and play in the meadow, while she licks the
tears of joy from his face
Then they both walk through Heaven's Gate together,
never again to be parted

Ian McMurdo